THERE MUST BE
MORE
THAN THIS

THERE MUST BE

MORE

THAN THIS

finding more life, love, and
meaning by overcoming your

SOFT ADDICTIONS

JUDITH WRIGHT

BROADWAY BOOKS / NEW YORK

TO BOB

who believed.

My living example of More.

It is through your love and

inspiration that I am more.

BROADWAY

PRINTED IN THE UNITED STATES OF AMERICA

BROADWAY BOOKS and its logo, a letter B bisected on
the diagonal, are trademarks of Random House, Inc.

Visit our Web site at www.broadwaybooks.com

First edition published 2003

Book design by Laurie Jewell

Library of Congress Cataloging-in-Publication Data
Wright, Judith.
There must be more than this: finding more life, love, and
meaning by overcoming your soft addictions /
by Judith Wright.—1st ed.
p. cm.
1. Self-actualization (Psychology)   2. Spiritual life.
3. Quality of life.   I. Title.

BF637.S4 W75 2003
158.1—dc21   2002035635

ISBN 0-7679-1339-6

3   5   7   9   10   8   6   4

CONTENTS

INTRODUCTION

As a child I was hungry—hungry for more than all the snacks and junk food I was stuffing into my mouth. No matter what I ate or what I did, it wasn't enough. The hunger persisted. I kept feeling that there must be more to life. I didn't know then that it was my spiritual hunger that needed feeding.

Growing up in a factory town, I didn't get many clues from others about how to meet spiritual hungers. Most people around me spent long hours zoned out on the assembly line. Upon leaving the plant, they'd grasp for ways to chase the tedium away: watching television, hanging out, comparing rumors of plant closings, or using other diversions.

It felt as if I lived in two worlds. In one, I had rich experiences and opportunities; my days were filled with dance, music lessons, camp, Girl Scouts, leadership in numerous clubs, and travel. I read a lot, rode my bike, and played with a diverse group of neighborhood kids. We wrote plays, acted them out, made costumes, sold tickets, and served refreshments. We held carnivals and played restaurant, shoe store, and grocery market. I set up lemonade stands, founded a revolving neighborhood library, and wrote a neighborhood newspaper as well as stories that my sister illustrated. Always first in my class, I poured myself into school activities and my studies. Yet, in my union town, doing well in anything other than sports meant little, with mediocrity valued over excellence. I was even scorned for winning state competitions and being a student leader. Despite the lack of recognition, when deeply engaged in these activities, I didn't feel so hungry.

In another part of my life, I would come home from school, plop my chubby self down in the recliner, flip on the television, and mindlessly eat bags of chocolate chip cookies and drink cartons of milk or chew my nails and lazily leaf through stacks of magazines during TV commercials. Zoned out, I drifted through the afternoons until I rallied myself to do homework or was called by friends to play.

When not deeply engaged in creative activities, or numbed by the TV, I felt empty and hungry. My heart hurt, though I wouldn't have been able to say it then in those terms. Waves of pain flowed through me. I often felt hollow or as if I were some kind of wispy ghost, barely existing. I knew something wasn't right but not what was wrong. I felt that life was supposed to be somehow different.

I had to remind myself that it wasn't just me. "Something" was missing. Acutely aware of the world around me, I sensed that something was "off." People didn't seem really happy or alive. They were in the house, but not "home"; busy, but not engaged; doing something that should be fun, but not looking happy; talking, but not making contact; gazing at newspapers or television, but uninvolved at deeper levels. Life was lonely in this world, full of activity without deep engagement—activities without aliveness, full of zoned-out spaces and zoned-out faces. It felt foggy, as if everyone were wrapped in cotton. I worried sometimes that I was the weird one and the world was fine, but deep inside I knew something was missing in the way people lived. I couldn't articulate *then* how it should be.

As an adult, I've found another way, and I'm eternally grateful for the path that has opened up to me. Relieved and joyful, I discovered that the "More" I had dreamt of as a child was real. I learned that most of us, locked in our routines, are denied More because we don't know it exists. Unconsciously, we believe that "this is all there is." As a result, we waste too much time and energy on television, shopping, self-pity, fantasizing, and other activities. We miss out on deeper, more meaningful lives. These time wasters become "soft addictions™": habitual activities or moods that numb our feelings, sap our life force, and lock us into a limbo of muted experience. These limiting habits and soft addictions prevent us from deeper satisfaction or spiritual fulfillment. We guide our lives by old unconscious, unexamined, limiting beliefs, rather than by loving truths that nourish and lead us to our greatest fulfillment.

Once recognized, these limiting beliefs can be challenged and replaced, and soft addictions can be managed. When we learn new behaviors and break through to higher levels of consciousness and love, we can then fulfill our deeper spiritual hungers. We can see beyond our superficial material wants. We feel connected to our deepest selves, others, and the universe, rather than connected just to the shopping channel or the Internet.

I want to share my excitement with you about what I am learning, how it feels to be awake, alive, conscious, and engaged. I hope reading this book helps you on your path of learning to live an inspired, exceptional life—nourishing your spirit rather than feeding your soft addictions. I eagerly share with you the evolution and ultimate vision that has helped me and many others.

MY SOFT ADDICTIONS

While I finally lost weight in college, food still had a powerful hold on my time and energy—I devoured recipes in newspapers and magazines and frequently fantasized about food. I used these and other soft addictions (biting my nails, procrastinating, zoning out over my textbooks) to push my feelings out of my awareness. I was thin but still didn't experience the More I was seeking. I drifted out of touch with who I was, what I might become, and the rich fulfillment life offered.

I married and then divorced, never finding what I discovered later was possible between two people. I think of my first marriage as a long date: full of activities, parties, hanging out, movies, and television, but no contact, communication, or shared purpose. I used soft addictions to blind myself to my ex-husband's harder addictions and hidden secrets. Numbed out and engaged in mindless activity and unguided by a higher purpose, we didn't foster what was best for either of us. I finally rallied, sought help, and found support. I shifted my behavior, and I ended the relationship when my ex refused to work on the relationship and grow with me. Gradually, I awoke to my spiritual hunger—how I longed to feel loved and connected to God, how I yearned to feel that I mattered, how I wanted to make a deeper difference in the world. Rather than mask this hunger by trying to fill up an empty hole with meaningless, anxious activities, I decided to do what I could to feed that hunger directly.

I discovered a deeper me underneath the soft addictions—someone who cared deeply, wanted more out of life, and had gifts and talents to develop and offer to the world. I learned to be with myself rather than avoiding myself with limiting habits and soft addictions. I started to experience my feelings more thoroughly rather than numb myself.

I learned to honor my feelings. I went toward them rather than running away. I began to add more nourishing foods, activities, and satisfying ways of being to my life. A dip in the hot tub felt more relaxing than drinking wine and it didn't negatively alter my consciousness or leave any yucky aftereffects. Belly-laughing with abandon, praying, and experiencing moments of joy felt better than getting high.

Spontaneous laughing, yelling, and even crying my guts

out in deep sobs brought me peace as no amount of unconscious, numbing behavior ever could. Learning to tell my deeper truths, avoiding secrets, and revealing myself felt scary—yet freeing. Reading great literature felt better than sitting dazed in front of the television. As I added nourishing behaviors, I noticed that I wasn't so attracted to my soft addiction routines. Their hold on me began to lessen.

Through my journey, I learned that these new, healthier behaviors could actually fill me up much better than food. It wasn't that I became indifferent to food—I still love creating exquisite meals and am quick to spot a sumptuous recipe—but I no longer obsess over food or even think about it much. Similarly, I watch little television, spend few precious minutes with daily newspapers and magazines, and never amble mindlessly through the mall. I love my work and find it exciting, nourishing, and fulfilling. I focus increasingly on spiritual development and personal growth and the joy of growing with others.

When I married my husband, Bob, I discovered the depth and joy of sharing life with someone on his own spiritual journey. Managing my soft addictions opened me to being in this loving, constantly evolving relationship. Sharing our quest has shown me the importance of aligning with higher purpose, being affirmed and supported, sharing like minds and hearts, and being with someone who wants the best for me.

In fact, my next big discovery was the hunger others had to share this journey with me. Today at the Wright Institute for Lifelong Learning, which Bob and I founded, I conduct workshops, guide pilgrimages to sacred sites worldwide, write, and create new ways of coaching and serving others. Although I'm very busy (sixty- to eighty-hour workweeks are common), I find time to work out, read three to five books weekly, go to movies, ride my bike through the countryside, cross-country ski, canoe, and walk in the woods. I plan recreation and renewal breaks. I spend a Sabbath day each week without work, when my husband and I read inspirational and holy writing, play, rest, re-create, sift through life priorities, and focus on our relationship with each other and with spirit. And because I accept and express my feelings, I'm more likely to cry instead of stay in the blues. I use my anger to trigger a change rather than feel sorry for myself.

MAKING MY ONE DECISION

Creating a life of More didn't happen overnight. It has been a journey of many milestones. As you'll see, the road to More is a series of highly conscious and deeply felt steps. The first and most important of these was what I call making my "One Decision." For me, making my One Decision meant taking a stand in my life for fullness and consciousness. Unwilling to live my life numbed out, I also didn't want others to live checked out. I made a commitment to be more awake and present, and to help others do the same.

Thankfully, ever since childhood, I had kept engaging fully in activities, doing well at school, and helping others in my work. I had challenging careers, including designing and running cutting-edge programs that helped adults with disabilities to attend college. I developed a national model program for children with disabilities and their families, wrote grants, did research, published, and worked with families at a university. But once I made the One Decision, I changed my work again. I started a personal and spiritual growth business, which allowed me to keep my commitment of helping others "awaken," too.

At the same time, my husband had a training business that helped people develop skills in areas of life such as leadership, relationships, and careers. We used to refer to his business as masculine and mine as feminine, but the differences were deeper. The people he served were terrific. Working with Bob and his talented staff, they would accomplish many goals and develop skills in intimacy, assertiveness, and relationships, but they wanted more. They flocked to my business for workshops I led to get this extra something—a sense of spirit, compassion, humor, deeper meaning, and a relationship with God, a higher power, or the universe.

In both of our businesses, we observed the difference between people who kept growing and those who did not. Those who stalled in their personal development often had counterproductive soft addictions that stood in the way of their growth and the life they said they wanted. They worked hard in our personal growth seminars to uncover feelings and let their emotions out, but then they frequently would return after a stimulating training weekend and indulge in soft addiction routines to numb what they had just unearthed. They would lose their momentum and the possibility of deepening their journey.

I looked at my own life and saw how I had shifted my behaviors away from numbing habits and what a difference it had made to the quality of my life. I saw that the net of routine was trapping them, just as it had once trapped me. At that point, we coined the term "soft addictions." We offered the first training in overcoming them in 1991. The response and the phenomenal results continue to grow.

WHAT IS THE MORE?

At this point, you've probably asked yourself this question. The answer varies from person to person, and you'll find ideas and tools throughout the book to help define the More for yourself. But in general we can say that we discover more life, love, and meaning on our journey through our commitment to pursue the greater More.

By meeting our deeper needs directly and releasing soft addictions, we are more fulfilled. By not spending so much time and money on insidious soft addiction routines, we have more time, energy, and resources to pursue more meaningful activities. We feel more awake, alive, and conscious. We spend more time discovering and developing our gifts and talents, making more of a difference in the world.

A thirty-something technology manager and father of three has been following the steps you will find in this book. He describes the life of More he found by breaking free from his soft addictions of television watching, overeating, and Internet surfing:

There is more hope and optimism in my life. I have a more positive outlook. I have more compassion for myself and less self-abuse. Little things are important. I get more done, take on more, and enjoy more. I am stepping up to more leadership, taking charge more, and becoming less judgmental. I have more awareness of and compassion for others. I spend more time on quality activities, and have more passion in my relationships—with my family and coworkers. I watch less TV, and instead, plan more and do more with my wife and children. I am in better physical shape and emotional condition. I experience greater urgency to enjoy what I do. I laugh more at myself. I feel more confident about myself in my career and I make a lot more money.

WHY DO WE LIVE A LIFE OF LESS?

If a life of More offers so much more of everything positive, then why do we live lives of less? There are many reasons for this. The seductive and insidious appeal of soft addictions, their easy availability, and their social acceptability are part of the reason. Soft addictions are woven throughout our culture and promoted in ways that both create and then fill the "need" we develop for them. Technological advances bring more diversions and possibilities. The very advances that promise us more time leave us less fulfilled. They are often the things that we use to zone out or aimlessly fill our time.

Yet, this does not fully tell us why these soft addictions are so prevalent and alluring. Why do people flee a life of More?

We often have mistaken beliefs that keep us from pursuing the More. We may not think that More is possible. We may not feel that we deserve More. We may fear our feelings or see them as an inconvenience. We haven't developed the skill to be with our deeper emotions or learned to use them as rich resources of information. We substitute numbing soft addictions for true comfort and self-care.

But the promise of More is worth facing and overcoming the fear. When we face our feelings, we learn to use the information they offer. We become more authentic, in touch with our world and ourselves. The temporary reprieve we have from numbing ourselves doesn't compare to the richness and adventure of a life of More.

WHAT TO EXPECT FROM YOUR JOURNEY

Learning to manage soft addictions and embrace the More has not been my experience alone. Hundreds of people at the Wright Institute have now made a similar journey, and you'll find their stories as well as mine in this book. Together we've been able to overcome our habitual behaviors and have learned to live increasingly exceptional lives. We support each other in our quest for conscious living—choosing less television, caffeine, shopping, excessive exercising, daydreaming, isolation, and the 101 other things that reduce consciousness. We celebrate deep relating, risk taking, truth telling, rest, full engagement, and other infinitely available nourishing acts of consciousness.

Over the years, the students in my workshops have helped me refine the process of overcoming soft addictions and finding more meaning. By taking this journey, they have created new ways to live lives of ever-increasing More. Our discoveries fall into eight key life skills:

1. Making your One Decision to live a life of More.

2. Identifying your soft addictions.

3. Minding your mind to break your denial and clean up your stinking thinking.

4. Discovering the Why of your soft addictions and cracking your own code.

5. Differentiating your hungers from your wants.

6. Developing a Vision.

7. Learning the Math of More to implement your Vision.

8. Developing support and accountability.

These eight skills are the keys uncovered by those who have chosen to lead exceptional lives at the Wright Institute for Lifelong Learning. They are the components of a proven process to fulfill spiritual hunger and increase consciousness and they can help you, too, to find more life, love, and meaning.

Throughout the book I'll talk about spirit, spiritual hunger, and God. I use these terms to reflect a broad concept of spirituality and God; they are not meant to represent any particular religion or spiritual tradition. At the Wright Institute, we serve people on all paths in living the More, be it religious traditions (Catholic, Protestant, Jewish, Muslim, Buddhist, or other) or a purely secular alignment with higher purpose. Please use these references as an opportunity to reflect on what fulfills your spiritual hunger and makes your heart sing. This could allude to a general spiritual sense, a particular religious tradition, a connection with God, Goddess, Buddha, Universe, Creator, your higher self, or higher principles such as love and truth.

The fact that you've picked up this book means that you are interested in finding More. While all of us have soft addictions, not all of us are willing to admit that they are a barrier to the life we deserve or a significant problem that we want to address. By reading this book, you make a positive statement and join many others who have made conscious living a reality. Many of the people at the Wright Institute have noted that recognition of their soft addictions was crucial for making the transition to conscious living. If they had not examined them, their fulfillment would have been limited. As you'll discover, your soft addictions contain enormous amounts of information about your deeper needs. Once we obtain this information and act on it, we are in a much better position to manage our soft addictions and live a life of More.

Though controlling soft addictions is a concrete benefit of this book, it is not the only one. Each step of the process brings with it tremendous self-knowledge. The information in each chapter is designed to prepare you for a lifelong journey, an awakening of your spirit that has been numbed by your addictions.

The initial chapters show you how we become locked into the routines and habits of soft addictions and lose sight of the more meaningful things life has to offer. We will explore how pursuit of the More provides a spiritually satisfying alternative to our myriad routines. To differentiate the illusion of "more"—more stuff, more money, more possessions—from the greater "More" I am addressing in this book, I will use a capital "M" when referring to the bigger More in life.

The second part of the book shows you a path you can follow toward the More. It provides a process for managing soft addictions as well as discovering and satisfying deeper hungers. It introduces you to the One Decision, teaches you to identify your particular web of soft addictions, and guides you in developing a vision for your life. These eight chapters lead you toward an increasingly conscious, authentic lifestyle.

The final chapters provide extra support and inspiration for your journey.

Throughout the book, you'll find tools, inspiring stories, and a wealth of ideas and information to help you on your journey. You will notice four types of sidebars scattered throughout the chapters:

"More-sels" are nuggets (morsels) of inspiration to encourage you on your journey.

"More to think about" invites you to reflect on the theme of the chapter.

"More to do" gives you a task to apply what you are learning about achieving the More.

"More alert" is a caution that alerts you to possible blocks or barriers to living the More.

People who embark on this journey may fear that they will have to quit all their addictions cold turkey. I want to assure you that this is not the goal, nor is it desirable in most cases. Most people change gradually. You can still watch television or exchange gossip and find the More you're seeking. On the other hand, you do need to become more aware of your patterns and create more positive choices. The process of overcoming your soft addictions is additive. When you add soul-satisfying activities to your life, a by-product is a natural reduction of soul-numbing activities. Consciousness is the key. If you want more out of life, then you need to practice being more aware of yourself in the moment. As you attune to the choices you face every day, you will naturally and easily grow in consciousness.

As I suspected when I was a child, there *is* another way. It's not a mere abstraction but a real alternative to the traditional way people exist. In the following pages, you'll find many examples of people already living lives of More.

HOW TO GET THE MOST OUT OF THE JOURNEY

I hope you'll be inspired to follow these steps to create a life of More. To get the most out of your journey, apply the material to your life and do the exercises. Just reading the book will serve you by raising your consciousness, but you won't create a life of More unless you take action. Although you can do this by yourself, many have found they are more likely to stick to it with support. Share the process with friends. Support makes for better follow-through, and developing support is one of the ways to have More in every aspect of life. Chapter 10 is filled with ideas for creating support for yourself, but you don't need to wait. You can find like-minded and like-spirited buddies, start a group of your own, be part of an on-line community, register to start a group in your area, attend a training, or even become a trainer yourself by logging on to my Web site at *www.there mustbemore.com*. You can ask questions and share thoughts with people who have been on the journey for a long time—people whose stories appear in these pages—and others who are just starting on their own personal journeys. You'll find chats, bulletin boards, quizzes, soft addiction computer games, Webcasts, and more to encourage and support you on your path. Support and inspiration are powerful ingredients of a life of More. You deserve to have all of the support in the world to create a life of More.

I.

IS THIS ALL THERE IS?

"We get into a rut. We play tennis, we go
to a movie, we watch TV, but I keep saying,
'John, there has to be more.'"

—CHRIS EVERT

all-time great women's tennis champion at the peak
of her career (while married to John Lloyd)

Many of us imagine that if we were world champions, we would feel complete. Yet, even champions wonder, "Is this all there is?" Being a world-class performer in a sport or discipline isn't the same as being a champion in life. Even at the top of their game, champions can feel hungry for more.

Luckily, mastery in life doesn't require us to be world-class athletes or CEOs of multimillion-dollar companies. We arrive at mastery in life when we rise above our soft addiction routines and create a life of More.

As much as we might want a life of meaning, our lives are often full but not fulfilling. At the end of the day, do you ever ask yourself:

Did I move toward my goals and vision today?
Did I make a positive difference in other people's lives?
How did I stand up for what matters most to me?
*What did I do that was emotionally or spiritually
   nourishing?*

How did I grow as an individual?

*How did I experience love in my interactions and
activities?*

If you rarely or never ask these questions, welcome to the club. Most of us don't consciously design our daily lives to be uplifting, meditative, or deeply meaningful. We are enmeshed in routines that range from stressful to escapist. These routines prevent us from effectively asking the big questions or from devoting ourselves to endeavors that answer them positively. We go through the paces, enjoying life in a minor key and tolerating its petty irritations. We fall into familiar, comfortable habits that leave us little opening for More.

See if you recognize yourself or anyone you know in the following behaviors. Review these scenarios and think about the similarities and differences in your own life.

You wake up after multiple hits on the snooze button and jump into a series of mad dashes—getting the kids to school, catching the train or driving through rush hour, getting to work on time, making a project deadline, arriving on time for a meeting, and then picking the kids up from school. Conversations with friends or fellow workers revolve around office politics, local news, sports, celebrities, television shows, or investments. The conversations tend to be brief and fragmented; they bounce from one subject to the next and rarely address feelings, especially deeply held or troubling ones.

Your free time—what little you have—is devoted to meeting unfulfilling, acquired needs. You *need* a grande mocha from Starbucks, to watch soap operas, to listen to a particular radio station, to read the sports pages, to check your e-mail, to work out. You have a fleeting thought that you are overdoing it but are unable to think of something more productive to do.

Work alternates between anxiety-producing moments and the accomplishment of moderately satisfying tasks. You finish a project and your boss or client likes it and you feel like you've accomplished something. This feeling, however, doesn't last, and it's not something you're particularly proud of or think about with great satisfaction.

At times, you watch the clock. You can't wait until lunchtime or until the end of the workday, even though lunch is nothing special and you don't have anything particularly exciting to do after work. You procrastinate and make excuses about why your project is late, yet you play computer games with your door closed. You yearn for vacations, new work, or retirement, thinking that *then* you will be happy.

At home, you hop to the needs of the family or you zone out. Perhaps you have a glass of wine or two to take the edge off the day. You channel-surf at night but don't remember later what you watched. You spend hours flipping through catalogues, coveting new outfits or nifty gadgets. You fantasize about various guys and gals, whether you're married or not.

Yes, this may be an exaggeration of a typical day in a typical life. But it's not as far from our reality as we might like to believe. If you're like most people, you recognize aspects of yourself in the examples depicted—activities and behaviors that we refer to as "soft addictions." Though they're seemingly harmless, and somewhat pleasurable, they are ultimately empty routines. In the back of your mind you might even suspect that these routines prevent you from experiencing a more meaningful, fulfilling life.

Why then doesn't everyone immediately shift their activities and break their routines to gain a more satisfying existence? Unfortunately, it's easier said than done. These routines are soft addictions, and they exert a powerful hold on us.

WHAT ARE SOFT ADDICTIONS?

Soft addictions can be habits, compulsive behaviors, or recurring moods or thought patterns. Their essential defining quality is that they satisfy a surface want but ignore or block the satisfaction of a deeper need. They numb us to feelings and spiritual awareness by substituting a superficial high, or a sense of activity, for genuine feeling or accomplishment.

Many soft addictions involve necessary behaviors like eating, reading, and sleeping. They become soft addictions when we overdo them and when they are used for more than their intended purpose. Soft addictions, unlike hard ones such as drugs and alcohol, are seductive in their softness. E-mailing, shopping, and talking on the phone seem like perfectly harmless, pleasurable activities while we're engaged in them. When we realize how much time and energy we devote to them, however, we can see how they compromise the quality of our lives.

Though I'm going to provide you with a list of common soft addictions, you should understand that an almost infinite variety exists. A soft addiction can be as idiosyncratic as any individual personality. While a universal soft addiction might be television watching, a more personal form might be doodling geometric figures or counting things for no reason.

Some people have difficulty differentiating an occasional behavior or fleeting mood from a soft addiction. If you watch television one hour per day, is it only a harmless habit, while if you watch three hours per day (the national average[1]), is it a soft addiction?

More to do

Rent the movie *About a Boy* for an eloquent example of a softly addicted life. The main character, played by Hugh Grant, lives a life centered around soft addiction routines until he discovers the More through his unlikely relationship with a lovable and nerdy preteen boy.

1. David G. Myers, *The American Paradox* (New Haven and London: Yale University Press, 2000), p. 200.

As a general rule, keep the following in mind: The motivation and the function of your behavior determine whether or not it's a soft addiction. For instance, television can be a window into new worlds, stimulating viewers with new ideas and leading them into meaningful pursuits—or it can be a means of escape. I know a woman who is very selective in what she watches, using television as a tool to learn about life in foreign cultures and to understand animal behavior. She employs television watching as a tool to gain knowledge. Another woman I know vegges out in front of the television daily, channel surfing and letting the programs wash over her. She leads a tough, hectic work life, and she mistakenly believes her viewing habits relieve her of stress. Rarely does she have a particular program she wants to watch or a real reason for watching it.

As you compare the two television watchers, the differences in motivation and function are clear. The first woman's motivation revolves around very specific learning goals; the second woman's motivation is to numb herself. The first woman uses television to enhance her life; the second woman uses it to escape from her life.

Sometimes, however, the line between soft addictions and productive activities is less clear. Here are a few clues to help you define this line and recognize that your behavior is a soft addiction:

Zoning out. One way of identifying a soft addiction is to ask if you zone out while you're doing it. When we are zoned out, we are not fully engaged. We may be checked out or have a "nobody's home" look on our face. Zoning out suggests that the goal of our activity is numbness. Although we're physically engaged in an activity, our mind is elsewhere. After the activity, we often don't remember what we've done, seen, or read. While this often happens when watching television, it can also occur while shopping, working, having superficial conversations, or doing other activities.

Avoiding feelings. Does a given activity or mood grant you a reprieve from your emotions, especially intense emotions? We avoid feelings by being numb, enhancing the feelings we like to the exclusion of others, or even wallowing in one unpleasant feeling to avoid another. Many of us are uncomfortable with our deepest feelings, whether positive or negative. We don't know how to deal productively with our sadness or anger (or, in some instances, with our joy), so we find an activity or a mood that facilitates an emotion-muting state, leaving us with subdued sadness, low-level anger, or other unsettled feelings.

Compulsiveness. Does an irresistible urge drive you to indulge a particular behavior or mood? Do you feel compelled to do, have, or buy something, even though you know you don't need it? This may be accompanied by a helpless, powerless feeling. You may be unable to stop or reduce the amount of time spent on a given activity. Though you may find some transient pleasure, you often don't feel good about yourself after engaging in it. You persist in following the routine, saying to yourself, *I'll never do this again.* Though you try to stop, you can't.

Denial/Rationalization. If you're defensive or make excuses for your behavior, chances are it's a soft addiction. Denial is a refusal to acknowledge and rationalization is an excuse or explanation we use to justify a compulsive behavior. Both blunt our self-awareness and lower our expectations of ourselves. To make our actions acceptable, we ignore, conceal, or gloss over the real motive or cost. Either we maintain that a habit isn't a problem or we rationalize why it's an acceptable or necessary way to spend our time. "What's so bad about a few cups of coffee?" is a typical rationalization. We may deny that the hours spent surfing the Net are a waste of time and energy. The impulse to deny or rationalize a routine suggests a soft addiction.

Stinking thinking. Related to denial and rationalization, "stinking thinking" is distorted thinking based on mistaken beliefs. Overgeneralizing, magnifying, minimizing, justifying, blaming, and emotional reasoning are some examples. Stinking thinking creates the funny rules and logic of soft addictions, such as "There are no calories if I eat standing up," or "I can't possibly work out if I've already showered." Woven throughout soft addiction routines, this type of thinking is addictive in itself. The distorted thoughts prompt indulging in a soft addiction in the first place and later let us justify the indulgence.

Hiding the behavior. Beware of habits that become guilty pleasures you seek to hide. Covering up the amount of time you spend on an activity or lying to others about how you frequently spend your time or your money are signs of soft addictions. In other words, you feel ashamed of what you're doing and that's why you want to hide it from others.

Avoiding feelings or zoning out are perhaps the most telling of these signs. Part of the allure of soft addictions is that they provide an escape from the pace and pressure of life. If we've had a tough day, we want to relieve the pressure. The same impulse that pushes people to have a drink rather than talk out tensions at the end of a hard day leads them to soft addictions.

Doing this is perfectly natural. We all need to zone out at times. Zoning out allows our unconscious mind to sort things out, giving us the downtime we need to regroup. It would be unusual to find anyone who didn't need to escape from his feelings at certain moments. The problem, of course, is when this becomes a way of life and soft addictions become deeply ingrained. We become like football players who have an injury but anesthetize themselves so they can get back in the game. As a short-term strategy, this may work. We convince ourselves that if we didn't have our soft addictions, we couldn't keep going to work, taking care of the kids, and generally keeping our life together. The danger to the football player, however, is that the underlying injury never gets treated and can even worsen. Similarly, we become accustomed to numbing ourselves and never consciously feeling any pain (or any intense emotion, for that matter). In this way, we become out of touch with our deeper self. We fail to meet deeper needs and move farther from our full potential. At certain moments, however, we glimpse how out of touch we are and ask, "Is this all there is?"

PEOPLE WHO ASK THE QUESTION

Dave, Sharon, and Lana are examples of individuals in the grip of soft addictions who recognize that something is missing in their lives. They realize that the low level of sustenance provided by their soft addictions is insufficient or comes at great cost. See if these stories remind you of yourself or someone you know.

Dave is an executive with a start-up company. Not only does he work late and on weekends, he has also significantly reduced the time he spends with his wife and two small children. Even worse, his wife complains that he's always distracted when he's at home with the family. At work, Dave downs cup after cup of coffee to stay awake and alert. He tells himself that his current situation is only temporary (though it's lasted over two years) and he'll be his old self when the company turns the corner. One night he was still at the office at ten o'clock, and he overheard a coworker calling his wife and talking sweetly to his children. Dave couldn't remember the last time he'd spoken so sweetly to his family. Deep inside himself, Dave wondered if he wasn't missing the point. For a moment, he experienced a sense of panic, a feeling that he had somehow devoted himself to the wrong cause.

Sharon is always on the move. Frightened of free time, she constantly busies herself. When she isn't at work, she's on the phone. When she isn't on the phone, she's at the gym. When she's not at the gym, she is going out to eat with any one of her numerous impersonal acquaintances. She dates people she doesn't like and rationalizes the dates as entertainment, although she complains to friends that there are no good men left. For a while, Sharon convinced herself that all this activity translated into a full, rewarding life. When she was younger, Sharon had hoped to make a difference in the world. When she moved to the city, she convinced herself that she was making a difference—she had a prestigious job with an advertising agency and frequented world-class restaurants. She was also active in rock-climbing clubs and environmental groups. A conversation with her sister about spirituality, however, caused her to wonder if she was simply doing many different things rather than making a real difference. She confessed, "I know I'm busy and leading a so-called glamorous life, but there are times I wish I could slow down and discover who it is I'm supposed to be." She closed up immediately, however, when her sister suggested meditation or even prayer.

Lana dramatizes her life. At the slightest urging, she'll entertain you with her tales of woe. Her car was stolen; her phone service was cut off because she didn't pay the bills on time; her root canal was the worst one ever; and she was fired from her last job because the company thought she was too outspoken. Lana relishes relating her nightmarish experiences and always has an excuse or explanation for why they weren't her fault. She fends off solutions with excuses. Lana tells entertaining stories, and she likes her stories as much as her audience does. It's only when she's alone and lacks an audience, however, that she perceives she's merely playing a role. It scares her that the most rewarding experience in her life is talking about her problems and that she derives little pleasure when things go well. From time to time, Lana worries that she sabotages her life in order to accumulate nightmarish tales. This frightening thought causes her to ask herself, *What am I doing with my life?*

Dave, Sharon, and Lana all have experienced an acute awareness of something missing from their lives. But they are so trapped in their soft addictions that it's difficult for them to search for what's absent. Dave convinces himself that all his hard work will pay off for his family, but he is dimly aware that his stress and misery in the pursuit of his work goals are driving his family away. Sharon lives a seemingly glamorous life but she fears looking too deeply to see what's missing. Lana's habit of turning her misfortunes into entertainment is so ingrained that she can't stand for things to go well. Their misguided, short-lived solutions of overwork, surface glamour, and drama are unconsciously geared to make the discomforting awareness, not the soft addiction, go away. Like most people, their soft addictions reduce their satisfaction.

Let's look at the range and type of addictions. While there is an infinite variety, I've tried to include the most common ones. Everyone has soft addictions. If you don't find one here that fits you, I hope this list inspires you to note the ones that have you in their grip.

THE TOP SOFT ADDICTIONS

Soft addictions fall into four different categories as reflected in the following list: activities, moods/ways of being, avoidances, and things. Some of the listed items may strike you as odd, trivial, or silly. They are not so silly if you're one of those people who uses them instead of dealing with the issues in your life. In Chapter 4 you'll discover more tools to identify your own soft addiction routines and learn how to recognize if something is a soft addiction or just a harmless pastime. For now, keep an open mind about all the listed addictions and place a check mark next to the ones you feel you're most vulnerable to. If you think of addictions that are not on the list, feel free to add your own.

Activities

While all of these activities are normal behaviors, any of them can become a soft addiction if it is overdone or used to zone out or avoid feelings. Think about whether you or anyone you know habitually overdoes these activities:

Media

Watching television
   Channel surfing
   Program junkie
Surfing the Internet
Participating in chat rooms
Checking investments
Checking weather, statistics, news
Reading magazines

Reading only one genre of novel, such as romance or mysteries
Listening to the radio
Checking e-mail
Playing computer games
Playing video games
Checking eBay

Buying/Shopping

Shopping
Collecting
Bargain hunting
Hanging out in the mall

Perusing catalogues
Clipping coupons
Cruising garage sales
Antiquing

Maintenance

Overeating
Overexercising
Glamorizing
Hygiene
Housekeeping

Being a pack rat
Caregiving
Sleeping too much
Nail biting

Physical Mannerisms

Hair twirling
Twitching, jiggling, picking

Gum chewing

Sexual

Flirting
Sexual obsessions
Phone sex
Pornography
Masturbating compulsively

Being a voyeur
Babe or dude watching
Being promiscuous
Leering
Fantasizing

Work

Overworking
Keeping busy

Overscheduling
Overcommitting

Risk Taking

Speeding
Gambling

Seeking danger
Making deals

Social/People

Name-dropping
Following celebrity news
Gossiping

Storytelling
Fantasizing/daydreaming
Lying

Other Diversions

Checking sports stats
Doing crossword puzzles

Playing card games

Moods/Ways of Being

Moods and ways of being can become soft addictions when they become habitual responses rather than genuine emotional responses to being upset. Think about the people you know who are habitually sarcastic or have high energy even when a situation doesn't warrant it. People who complain frequently, crack jokes, or act cool much of the time may be using that way of being as a habitual way to distance themselves from their deeper feelings.

Being sarcastic
Being cranky/irritable
Indulging in self-pity
Being "in the know"
Being a drama king or
    queen
Always being happy; always
    "on"
Being a Pollyanna
Chameleonlike behavior
Acting like a sad sack
Moping

Blaming
Looking good
Complaining
Constantly trying to please
    people
High energy
Jokester
Perfectionism
Fanaticism
Being argumentative/con-
    flictual
Acting cool

These mood soft addictions differ significantly from clinical mood disorders. The former are "normal" reactions that turn into numbing habits while the latter are "abnormal" conditions that often require therapy and treatment.

Avoidances

At first glance, it may be hard to see avoidance as a soft addiction. After all, avoidance involves *not* doing something. But not doing something, evading, or minimizing can be ways to keep you checked out and unengaged. Escaping can become a habitual response to upset and can feel just as compulsive as more active behaviors.

Procrastinating	Playing the victim
Isolating	Hypochondria
Being late	Phobias
Playing dumb	Stonewalling
Living in clutter	Being too busy
Playing helpless	Oversleeping/napping

Things—edible and consumable

Habitually overindulging in things from fancy chocolates to designer coffees can be a soft addiction. Consistently going for a "hit" when you are having feelings may signal a substance addiction. You may not have considered gadgets or designer clothing as being possibly addictive things, but if you must have the latest thing and feel incomplete without it, you may be vulnerable to this type of addiction. If you become anxious when your supply runs low or runs out, you're likely addicted. You may spend time planning on using a given substance. It might even take on the form of a ritual.

Sugar	Cigarettes
Chocolate	Gadgets
Fast foods	Designer clothes
Carbohydrates, high-fat foods, etc.	Collectibles
	CDs
Coffee	DVDs
Snack foods	Brand-name merchandise

LIVING A SOFTLY ADDICTED LIFE

Many times, soft addictions come in clusters and doing one encourages another. Someone might overindulge in snack foods while zoned out watching television. Another might bite his nails when jittery from too much caffeine. Someone who has the addiction of acting cool and aloof might also be addicted to gadgets and designer clothes. Mood addictions can pave the way for substance or activity addictions and vice versa.

See if you can identify the soft addictions that Brenda has and their impact on her life in the following vignette.

Brenda shifted careers to take a more meaningful job at a growing, socially conscious company. Overwhelmed by the responsibilities and not feeling on top of her workload, she came in early one morning, skipping her workout. She then felt burdened and sorry for herself and called a girlfriend to complain. After that, Brenda was really behind, so she skipped lunch. Ravenously hungry in the afternoon, she grabbed a bag of

> ### More to think about
>
> The average household has the television on seven hours a day. The average person watches three to four hours of TV a day. The average child spends more time watching TV than she does in school—up to 20,000 hours. By the time the average person reaches age fifty, he will have spent seven years of his life watching TV.
>
> DAVID G. MYERS
> *THE AMERICAN PARADOX* (NEW HAVEN AND LONDON: YALE UNIVERSITY PRESS, 2000)

her favorite chips from her stash. She mindlessly munched in front of her computer. Feeling fried, she tried to write a creative ad to hire help and spent three hours writing nothing of substance as she stared at the computer screen. Frantic, she then scrambled for something to do to feel more fulfilled and decided to clean out the drawers of her assistant's desk. Already late meeting her fiancé for a scheduled dinner, she blew off his concern with a distracted generalization about a bad day. She complained about a coworker as she devoured the whole breadbasket and wondered what to order for dessert. She also wondered why she wasn't feeling fulfilled at her new, meaningful job.

In Brenda's day, we see all four categories at work:

Activities: busywork
Avoidances: procrastination, being late, avoiding intimacy
Things: salty snack foods, carbohydrates, sugar
Moods/Ways of Being: self-pity

THE PARADOX AND POSSIBILITIES OF OUR TIME

Brenda might have struggled with some of these soft addictions if she had lived in an earlier era, but the odds are that they would not have been so multifaceted and pervasive. Soft addictions reflect the age in which we live, an age of paradox. The world we live in facilitates both soft addictions and spiritual enlightenment. The opportunities for fulfillment and meaning are equaled by the opportunities for creatively wasting time.

Many forces come to bear in our era that make us particularly vulnerable to the allure of soft addictions—the cumulative effect of our increased technology, our spotlight on wealth, redefining the "good life" materially rather than by our own goodness, the increase in disposable income, our need-for-the-new faddish society, the proliferation of institutionalized gossip, and the emphasis on quick fixes rather than engaging in thoughtful solutions to complex problems. We move faster and farther, feeling like we are going nowhere. We earn more, buy more, do more, and feel like we are living less. Time-saving devices are taken for granted as we move at an ever-quickening pace, complaining that we have no time. Bigger isn't necessarily better and more sometimes creates less—this is the paradox of our time. When we become trapped in this paradox and are content to do less with more, we fall prey to our soft addictions.

> More-sel
>
> "The paradox of our time . . . We have more conveniences but less time . . . We drink too much, smoke too much, spend too recklessly . . . read too little, watch TV too much, and pray too seldom. We have multiplied our possessions, but reduced our values . . . We've learned how to make a living but not a life."
> —GEORGE CARLIN

In an era when there's so much opportunity for a great life, people ask *Is this all there is?* with more fervor. We possess greater opportunities to fulfill our spiritual hungers but are confronted with more distractions—a dazzling array of seemingly important pursuits. Because of all the books, workshops, and other vehicles devoted to the subject of spirituality, consciousness has been raised for many of us. Yet because of the proliferation of video games, cultural fixation on celebrity gossip, and "reality-based" television shows, our consciousness has been similarly lowered.

Consider the tremendous power and potential of the Internet—the ability to democratize information, the possibilities of connectivity, the opportunity to discover values and appreciate diversity and demolish boundaries. The notion of global consciousness is utopian, but the Internet is a medium that can bring that dream closer to reality. Given all of this, it is staggering that one of the most frequent uses of the Internet is for visiting pornography sites.

Our challenge is to reconcile the paradox of more leading to less. This requires learning to distinguish between soft addictions and meaningful activities, between escapist entertainment and forums for self-discovery. We live in a time where the lines blur. We're vulnerable to style over substance, the appearance of energy rather than the reality. The sophistication of soft addictions and their marketing create the illusion that they're meaningful, enriching endeavors. We celebrate our "connectedness" as we spend hours buying and selling trivial objects on eBay. Just as significantly, the rising level of stress most of us are under makes soft addictions seem necessary. We feel we "need" to get away and watch television to escape the stress. Some outlets are inherently positive while others are limiting, but all can easily become vehicles of avoidance. To avoid being trapped, we must be aware of the paradoxical nature of our society and the challenges it presents.

WHY WE YEARN FOR SOMETHING MORE

Without awareness, we're easily confused about what's important in life. We fool ourselves into believing that numbness is good. It's amazing, therefore, that some of us are able to rise above our numbing soft addictions, refusing to drift in a moderately satisfying haze. How are we able to muster the consciousness to ask, *Is this all there is?* if we're locked into routines that provide the buzz we're seeking?

There are many superficial answers to this question, but the deepest answer is that at the core we're all inherently conscious, even spiritual people. We all have a higher, spiritual itch that needs to be scratched. That itch is more powerful than the numbing power of our soft addictions. Though we may be able to ignore it in the short term, our higher yearning eventually breaks through in moments of crisis, trauma, loss, or even death. For a while, however, we may convince ourselves that soft addictions are all there is. For a time, we may fall under the sway of the cynics and hedonists among us and tell ourselves that we're just not spiritual people or assume that the pleasures of life are to be found on the surface.

If we're lucky, we're not jolted out of our routines by a tragic event, like a death in the family, that makes us ask the bigger questions. We may

More-sel

"There must be more to life than having everything."
—MAURICE SENDAK

meet someone who lives a spiritually focused life and seems to derive more satisfaction from how he spends his time; he inspires us to ask whether we could be like that, too. Or we may read a book or attend a workshop that opens our eyes. Or it may simply be a flash of clarity that magically arrives, a sudden epiphany that allows us to feel strongly that there is something we're missing.

It's possible that this epiphany comes at the end of a wild-goose chase for meaning. People labor under the illusion that if they obtain more money or more objects, they will be happy and satisfied. Most believe that if they achieve society-approved goals—getting married, having a family, living in a dream house, going on nice vacations, getting promoted, achieving status, having money—they will enjoy a meaningful life. While there certainly is meaning in work, marriage, and family, they are only part of the More. Many of us grow dissatisfied with our lives and search in the wrong places and in the wrong ways for alternatives. In fact, some people escalate their soft addictions, trying new, superficial activities in an effort to feel better.

More to think about

Recall two events in your life—one tragic, the other transcendent—and reflect on what you felt about your life at the time. Did the tragic event give you a sense, however brief, that you had been wasting time? Did the transcendent event provide a vision of what your life might be?

For most, it's only at the end of this futile search that we start to understand that we need to begin a different type of search. All of us, whether we know it or not, have experienced moments of transcendence. Just about everyone has stood spellbound at sunset, reveled in the feeling of wet dew on the morning ground, witnessed the miracle of a child being born, or experienced a burst of dynamic creativity. This taste of life's possibilities stays with us, no matter how locked into our routines we may be. Powerful memories of conscious moments can break through even the most numbing soft addiction. Of course, some of us immediately rationalize the memory. We convince ourselves that we can't re-create it, that this transcendent moment resulted from being in the right place at the right time and won't come again.

Underneath all the rationalizations and soft addictions, however, resides a sense that we could be living a life that matters much more. The sense may exist at a subconscious level, but eventually it becomes conscious, and we start to wonder if we were put on earth for a purpose and even if we might have a noble destiny to fulfill. It's at this point that we often begin transitioning away from our soft addiction routines toward a life of contribution and meaning.

FROM SOFT ADDICTIONS TO A LIFE OF MORE

We each need to define and discover the More for ourselves as individuals, and, by the end of this book, you will have received important knowledge and tools to help you create your own personal vision and action plan for the pursuit of More. The More, you'll see, is what we want carved on our tombstone. Who would want their tombstone to read "Here lies Susan. She bought a lot of stuff"?

Jackie will have a more inspiring inscription on her tombstone, though it wasn't until recently that she could say that. Jackie used to be a mall rat. She spent her Saturdays wandering around malls meeting people she called friends, sometimes buying things but mostly just looking. She also watched tons of television and read the newspaper compulsively each morning. Karaoke and drinking were her idea of celebrating. She spent her remaining free time obsessing about food. Though Jackie weighed in the normal range, she would think about what she was going to eat and when, constantly reading cookbooks and planning what she was going to eat so that she could have something to look forward to.

When Jackie arrived at the Wright Institute, she talked about an emptiness in her routines. As hooked as she was on the mall, the newspaper, television, and especially her food obsessions, Jackie had become increasingly dissatisfied. She said she felt as if she were "biding her time, waiting for something to happen."

Over a period of months, Jackie used the process described in these pages to find her More. In making the transition to a new way of living, Jackie redirected her time and energies. She still reads the newspaper, but mostly to keep herself aware of what's going on in the world. She watches television much less and never randomly—she only sits down and watches programs that she has a particular interest in. Similarly, Jackie goes to the mall when she needs to make a specific purchase. Obsessing about food no longer grips her: she has other things to look forward to besides her next meal.

Jackie freed her time and energy for more meaningful pursuits. She now begins her mornings with uplifting music and has started to read books, especially insightful fiction and books about the soul. She developed deeper relationships with old friends and formed new, meaningful relationships. She turned from a follower in her office into a change agent, investing in the success of others. She spends more time going for walks in beautiful places, and she meditates during those walks.

Jackie finds the More in every moment. It's not that every moment is great or that she doesn't feel pain and sadness. In fact, she feels both pleasure and pain more intensely. But when Jackie experiences tough times, she has the internal resources to deal with them. She has a tremendous reservoir of inner strength and serenity to draw upon. Not a day goes by without joyous moments. She finds it in music, mentoring colleagues, or breathing the fresh air on a crisp fall morning. No longer does Jackie feel as if she is in limbo. Instead, she understands that her time has arrived and that she is taking advantage of the possibilities that life offers.

Like Jackie, you, too, can create a life of More. You can become a champion of life by applying the processes and exercises of this book. You are on your way to discovering the promise of More.

2.

THE PROMISE OF MORE

"Can't you see, I want my life to be something
more—than just long."
—From the musical *Pippin*, book by Roger O. Hirson;
music and lyrics by Stephen Schwartz

We all hunger for more in life, consciously or unconsciously. Some of us may not be aware of this hunger or may only sense it in rare moments of consciousness, but it's there. We may want more love, enjoyment, or fulfillment. We may wish to make more of a difference, have a greater sense of meaning, or gain a greater sense of peace. We might even feel a desire to connect with spirit or to be part of a larger whole. For some, it's a purely religious search for God, while for others it's a more general impulse for connectedness.

Regardless of the specifics, we all want More. Our soft addictions, though, mask this hunger for greater connection and meaning. As we numb ourselves or jump from routine to routine, we move out of contact with our deeper feelings and we settle for less. Soft addictions sap our time, energy, and emotions, leaving us feeling diminished and confused about what More there could be. Throughout this book, you'll learn ways to diminish the hold your soft addictions have on you. In this chapter, you'll learn more about the promise of what awaits when you do.

FROM NOT WANTING ENOUGH
TO WANTING MORE

You've probably made at least one of the following statements (out loud or to yourself) or heard others say them:

"Is this all there is?"

"Sometimes I feel like I'm wasting my life."

"I'm just going through the motions."

"I want to make a difference."

"I don't want to continue leading a superficial life."

"I just want to feel deeply connected to another person."

"I wish I could discover my purpose for being on this planet and fulfill it."

"I want to bring God into my life."

"I long to be part of the universe, to be in harmony with something larger than myself."

"I feel empty inside."

"There must be more."

As these statements suggest, the hunger for More manifests in a variety of ways. We each express our More uniquely because of our different issues, lessons, purposes, and even different soft addictions in our lives. We start out in a personal place, struggling to emerge from our sleep of limited consciousness maintained by soft addictions. We may begin by searching for more meaningful ways to live our lives, or we may begin by seeking deeper relationships. But ultimately, the More translates into a spiritual journey or a path of higher purpose for all of us.

Students don't always come to the Wright Institute seeking "more in life." Rather, they usually come to achieve a specific goal or to solve a particular problem. They may want to have a better relationship, become a better leader, or get a promotion. They may have problems they want to solve such as earning more or wanting to get out of a bad job situation or relationship. Perhaps they feel lonely and want to find a life partner. Often they think that their unhappiness is because they want too much in life and should settle for less. But once engaged on the path of More, they find that they did not want enough. Beyond just solving a problem or reaching a goal, there is a life of so much more.

Invariably, it was their limiting, unconscious beliefs and feelings that kept them from desiring More. They may have felt they didn't deserve More or may not have believed in an abundant universe. Perhaps they didn't consider the possibility of a loving God who wants them to have a rich and abundant life. For whatever reason, they don't initially see the unlimited possibilities of a life of More.

Katie was typical. She couldn't imagine there was More to life. She had a kind, handsome husband, two delightful children, and a business that allowed her to dabble in many exciting arenas. As a child of immigrant parents who eked out a living in Eastern Europe, she had more than she or her family could ever have imagined.

Katie was also overweight, underexercised, and overscheduled. She bit her nails, sucked up coffee, and spent long hours trying to unravel the dramas of family and friends. She couldn't imagine taking time for herself; there was too much to do. She resisted her friends' idea of hiring an assistant, feeling that she should simply be more efficient. Inside, Katie felt she already had so much and had achieved so much in her life that she couldn't imagine being entitled to More.

Katie initially came to the Institute with a supervisory problem that she was able to resolve in a short time. But once exposed to the possibility of More through coaching, courses, and the examples of the lives of other students, it didn't take Katie very long to expand her vision. She wanted More—more help and support, a more genuine sense of connectedness with family and friends, a deeper sense of service in her work, and more meaning in her everyday experiences. She hired an assistant, stopped dramatizing, and spent more time caring for herself and focusing on the parts of her work that fed her soul.

Like Katie, my students usually solve their initial problem or achieve their initial goals very quickly. Finding that there is More available to them in life, they begin to want it all.

FINDING MORE LIFE, LOVE, AND MEANING

What is the More they discover? It has many faces, as we'll see, but in every case, the quest for More leads to finding more life, more love, and more meaning.

More Life

We all yearn to have a full life, to take advantage of all life has to offer. "Life" is the word we use to describe the basic force that animates us. Cultures from Hindu to Christian occupy themselves with the mastery of it. Hindu saint Swami Muktananda felt becoming fully alive to be his greatest accomplishment. Christ is quoted as having said, "I come that they may have life and have it more abundantly."

When we are awake and aware, we experience more of life. We see life as a sumptuous banquet. We live bigger lives, not just limiting ourselves to the comfortable or familiar. Constantly growing and expanding, we have an increaing capacity to meet life. Our senses become more acute, our hearts open, and we are receptive to more experience. Rather than feeling deadened and shut down, we feel alive, vibrant, and vital. We live life to the fullest. As Norman Vincent Peale said, we touch life at more points: "What is it to be alive? A man who touches life,

More-sel

"Life is a banquet, but most poor suckers are starving to death."

FROM THE MUSICAL *MAME*, BY JEROME LAWRENCE AND ROBERT E. LEE; MUSIC AND LYRICS BY JERRY HERMAN say, at one hundred points is twice as alive as a man who touches it at only fifty points."

More Love

We don't need to look at love theologically to know that we all long to feel special and beloved, as well as to give love. We yearn to know that we matter, and we want to feel deeply connected with others. When we are stuck in our addiction routines, we are often too zoned out to notice our longing or summon this loving part of ourselves. We need to be present, conscious, and in touch with our emotions to give and get more love. Soft addictions reduce our very presence. If we are not all there, there is less of us to love. Our most essential self, our unique and caring self that loves and deserves to be loved, is hidden in the haze of soft addictions.

When we dedicate ourselves to pursuing More, we commit to accepting ourselves and our experiences instead of numbing them. This enhances self-love and compassion. We become people we respect and value. Treating ourselves with more care, we begin to receive from ourselves the love we crave. We make ourselves available to be really seen, cared for, and known by others, warts and all.

More Meaning

We long to extract more meaning from everyday actions. Meaning is defined by intention, purpose, and significance, the opposite of just going through the motions. When we live a life of More, we imbue our everyday activities with our values, and we fill our lives with more purpose. Perhaps you've expressed this need at some point by saying, "What is my purpose?" or "What am I doing this for?" None of us wants to sleepwalk through life, though that's exactly what we do when we become enmeshed in soft addictions. When we create a life of More, as you'll learn to do in this book, we have a life compass that gives not only direction but also meaning to all we do. We sense that we are fulfilling our destiny.

LIVING THE MORE

Byron did not have an epiphany that led him to his More. Rather, his discovery came gradually as he addressed his vague dissatisfactions. At first, Byron didn't know what to make of these feelings. As a manager in a health-care related field, he was well compensated, and he felt good about how his work helped people lead healthier lives. He also had a steady girlfriend, and they were talking about marriage. Despite it all, he came to the Institute saying, "There must be more than this." He yearned for more life, love, and meaning.

Byron was locked into his routines, and for a number of years he had allowed himself to sink into them and submerge his feelings of dissatisfaction. One of his soft addiction routines involved obsessively exercising and dieting; he spent enormous amounts of time and energy at the health club and shopping for the narrow range of foods he considered acceptable. Another soft addiction was sarcasm. Certainly, everyone is sarcastic at times. Used sparingly, it can be a healthy, tension-releasing trait. Byron, however, reflexively used sarcasm to avoid dealing with and revealing his feelings. He had gathered a fast-living, high-tech, low-touch group of friends who appreciated his sarcasm and returned it in kind. They weren't people who were particularly warm

> ## More-sel
>
> "I want to be thoroughly used up when I die . . . for the harder I work, the more I live. I rejoice in life for its own sake. Life is no brief candle to me. It is a sort of splendid torch, which I've got a hold of for the moment and I want to make it burn as brightly as possible before handing it on to future generations."
>
> —GEORGE BERNARD SHAW

and open. There was a lot of partying but very little mean-ingful connection. Their get-togethers were more like es-capes than true celebrations.

If Byron had tried to be more real with his friends, they would have made fun of him. They placed a high priority on appearance, and this priority drove Byron to focus much of his attention on shopping for the right kind of clothes and gadgets. Byron's weekend ritual was to work out with friends at the club, go shopping at certain stores, and then have a few drinks at their favorite bars before dinner. His empty feelings continued to grow.

When Byron came to the Institute, he talked about be-ing involved in "half-satisfying" relationships at work, at home, and with his friends. He said he did not want to have the same relationship his parents had, one marked by cold compromises and half-truths. He wanted more meaning than he saw in his father's drudgery at work. For Byron, his More in life revolved around connection. He longed for more truth, honesty, and intimacy in his relationships. He wanted to feel more deeply connected to others, especially his girlfriend.

Over time, Byron achieved this More. He and his girlfriend enrolled in classes at the Institute and learned how to live more conscious, con-nected lives. Not only did their rela-tionship deepen, but Byron also found himself making new friends with whom he could be more open, expressive, and genuine. He risked more. Sure, he got hurt, but his re-ward was the glow of warmth and mutuality often found in his encoun-ters. His soft addictions—shopping, exercising, dieting, sarcasm—gradu-ally diminished in importance. He began to use his free time differently; rather than club hopping and shopping,

More to think about

Think about people, whether acquaintances or public figures, who live lives of More—more life, love, and meaning. How would you describe their lives? Observe examples of lives of More so that you can begin to picture it for your-self.

he coaches a softball league for at-risk kids in the neighborhood.

At work, he is a more effective, caring, and empowering manager; he sees the meaning in helping employees do their best. Byron still works out and displays his sarcastic wit on occasion, but these activities no longer drain his energy and time or prevent him from exploring his feelings and spirituality. He marvels daily at the richness of his relationship with his now fiancée. They are joined in the pursuit of full aliveness, learning to love and live with purpose and meaning.

FEELINGS, CONSCIOUSNESS, AND ENERGY: THE DYNAMICS OF MORE

Learning to live the More, Byron became more conscious of the people around him—and more able to experience his emotions and to unleash more energy. As we increase our ability to feel, be conscious and be energized, we naturally and effortlessly generate More. When we master these dynamics, we automatically generate life, love, and meaning.

More Feelings/Emotions

Living a life of More means allowing ourselves to feel our pleasure and pain. Feelings and emotions are there to guide us: to correct missteps, move away from our pain, and move toward greater pleasure. When we live a life of More, we become more able to experience our feelings honestly and deeply, and this gives us greater information to act on. We learn and grow more when we feel our full range of emotions—from love, joy, and bliss to anger, sadness, and fear. We become more alive and genuine.

As I've emphasized, soft addictions numb our feelings. If we're stressed about some aspect of our life and we escape by shopping, we fail to notice the feeling and respond effectively to the stressor. It is as if we are anesthetized. If we're angry with our spouse and we distract ourselves from this scary emotion by turning on the television, we fail to address the issue and we deaden ourselves to each other.

At some point, though, we recognize that by numbing our feelings, we're not being genuine. By avoiding fear, we become less than we could be. We're afraid of showing our spouse our hurt or anger because we think, *If he saw that side of me, who knows what he'd do?* Certainly there are times when it's necessary to mask our feelings, but if we don't drop that mask to ourselves, we're living a false life—a life out of touch with the feelings that guide us to More.

The hunger for genuineness is powerful. When we honor our feelings, we follow a reliable guide to right action. Fear and anger guide us to move away from hurt and danger, remove a painful stimulus, set a boundary, or make a change. If we're joyous, we know we're on the right path and should continue or do even more. Learning to heed the information our emotions provide and becoming more expressive are skills of More, skills in being our truest selves.

The More, therefore, is a desire to know ourselves and be real. Most people sense they're only playing a part in life rather than being totally themselves. Living the emotional More allows us to experience greater intimacy with others and ourselves.

More Consciousness

Imagine life in a mild haze. After two or three drinks, you experience a buzzed, gauzy feeling. Or if you're moderately nearsighted or farsighted, consider what it would be like without your contacts or glasses. Or summon the feeling you have at the dentist when he gives you Novocain.

These conditions diminish our awareness and are analogous to how we feel in the grip of soft addictions. We've numbed, muted, shaded, and blurred our awareness of the world around us and inside. We don't notice things. We miss how our spouse's mood changes or we fail to note our feelings about people and situations. More significant, the consciousness-muting power of soft addictions keeps us from experiencing many of the positive things around us. We barely acknowledge a lover's admiring glance or we ignore a glorious sunset. Soft addictions shield us from the immediacy of the moment, and they prevent us from inhabiting it fully.

We are all aware of how short life is, and we want to make each moment count. More alertness, awareness, aliveness, and sensitivity transform our internal and external worlds. It's said that lifetimes can be lived in a moment, and while that can be hyperbole, being highly conscious does deepen the meaning of every moment, making life richer.

People who pursue consciousness report that they notice many things inside and out that they previously missed. Without consciousness, life just happens; we are only dimly aware of the forces that cause us and those around us to do what we do. More consciousness brings these forces to our attention. We understand more, and more awareness allows us to take control and create our own path.

> ## More to do
>
> What do you wish you could experience more fully? Is there something good in your life you haven't experienced? Let yourself feel it. Smile in gratitude.

More Energy

When we experience more of the vital life force that courses through us, we have more energy. Not only do we have greater power and stamina, we exude vitality.

In the movie *Invasion of the Body Snatchers*, quite the opposite happens. An alien life-form takes over people's bodies and souls. While people look and act as they did before they were taken over, they lack spirit. Therapists refer to people like this as having "flat affect." They're missing the energy or animated quality at the heart of being human. I'm not suggesting that soft addictions turn people into zombies. Yet, they do rob us of our energy.

Look around you the next time you're in a public place. How many people appear engaged, alive, and animated? How many seem like they're shut down or checked out?

As we open to our feelings and consciousness, we unleash our inner power. Stopping soft addictions takes the dampers off and we experience more aliveness and engagement. People who experience this energizing More tap into the life force. They seem to radiate energy. They act and feel vibrant. They take more risks, pursue learning, and, ultimately, have more life.

> ## More-sel
>
> "Energy creates energy. It is by spending myself that I become rich."
>
> —SARAH BERNHARDT

TRANSLATING THE MORE INTO A HIGHER-QUALITY LIFE

We've seen that the More means finding more life, love, and meaning, and more feelings, consciousness, and energy. In truth, the aspects of the More are infinite, but here are just a few more:

More time, money, and resources. Not wasting resources on soft addiction routines leaves more time and money for more meaningful, consciously chosen uses.

More of a difference. We use our gifts to make a contribution to the world, for loved ones or the larger universe.

More possibilities. No longer in a rut, life opens up infinite options.

More passion. Our energy is freed up for what we really care about. Life flows more fully through us.

More fulfillment and satisfaction. By developing ourselves and applying ourselves fully to whatever we do, we feel fulfilled. As we author our lives and live with more positive intent, we experience true satisfaction.

More quality of experience. Our everyday activities become more purposeful and are imbued with deeper meaning.

More flow. With effort, we can experience what Mihaly Csikszentmihalyi calls "Flow" in his book of the same name— optimal experiences where we are consciously absorbed in what we do, rather than mindlessly distracted.

More truth and genuineness. Without denial or masking the truth, we learn to live life revealed instead of hidden. We develop the courage to tell the truth, receive the truth, and deal with the truth.

More connection and intimacy. Becoming our real selves, we know ourselves more fully so others can know our real selves. We can experience intimacy, dropping our masks and meeting underbelly to underbelly. Revealed and open, we can touch and be touched.

More to think about

Is there something in your heart you'd like to express to a friend or loved one, an untold truth? Picture yourself opening up to tell them.

More creativity. Enhanced consciousness opens up your mind to new avenues and possibilities. Our artistic skills flourish and our problem-solving and imaginative abilities increase.

More self. Increasingly aware of our motivations and feelings, we are not just unconsciously reacting to life around us. We develop more depth and substance, and come to know ourselves more fully.

More God, more sense of spirit. We develop a growing spiritual awareness that we're not alone and that we're surrounded by spirit. The More can mean seeing life as a sacred journey where each moment is imbued with the divine.

And, there is more. There is all this, but the very nature of More is that there is also always More to discover.

DIFFERENTIATING YOUR DEEPER MORE FROM YOUR SURFACE MORE

You may not readily know what you are missing or how your soft addictions keep you from it. Even if you see clearly the greater More you want, it helps to start naming and describing the More in words.

Try this exercise to help you claim what your More might be. Look at the following two lists. List A contains the aspects of More we've discussed in this chapter. List B consists of the things we often mistake for the greater More. Use List A to stimulate your thinking about the spiritual hungers you most want to satisfy. Use List B to eliminate or reduce the power of the surface wants that don't satisfy these spiritual hungers. There is nothing wrong with wanting more money or more clothing. It's just that having those things won't lead you to the bigger More of life. Seeing the two lists side by side can put into perspective how unlikely material things are to help you achieve your longing for a more meaningful life.

> ### More to think about
>
> If someone were to ask you, "What's missing from your life?" how might you respond? What do you want More of?

A: DEEPER MORES	B: MISTAKEN/ SUPERFICIAL MORES
More love	More money
More life	More house
More creativity	More caffeine
More adventure	More power
More knowledge	More media
More beauty	More avoidance
More peace	More oversleeping
More meaning	More stuff
More feelings	More possessions
More consciousness	More diversions
More energy	More fame
More connection	More vacations
More direction	More car
More truth and genuineness	More image
More self	More status
More of a difference	More escapes
More God/spirituality	More clothing

Which of the Mores on the A list resonate with you? Write them down and note what matters to you or touches you (or verbalize it to someone you trust). If your articulation of the More feels right, begin right now to consciously make it a greater focus for yourself. Think about it daily. By being aware of your More, realizing it will be that much closer. If none of the items on List A seems right, feel free to generate your own More. Don't worry if your description of the More seems unusual or highly personal. There is no ideal More. We are

More alert

Be aware of these blocks to creating More:

Not wanting enough

Confusing more stuff with More

Being stuck in the sticky web of soft addictions

Fear of More

Fear of risk and change

all unique human beings and we all have our own special conceptions of what it is that will satisfy the deeper hunger within.

WHAT DOES THE MORE LOOK LIKE?

As you might expect, More means different things in different situations. At work it may mean a richly satisfying job, while at home it could involve more beauty and creativity, warmth, community, and inspiration. Spiritually you may want more peace or love, or to experience transcendence when you meditate. The More of relationship can mean partnership, harmony, better co-parenting, or touching deeply. Let's envision scenarios of the More in common situations—at work, at home, in relationships, in our spirituality, and during tough times.

What Is More at Work?

When we live the More in our jobs, work is no longer relegated to a series of tasks tied to the clock. The More pervades everything we do. Though every task may not radiate obvious meaning, purpose permeates all you do. No longer are you mindlessly going through a checklist. Instead, phone calls, letters, and meetings take on greater significance and urgency. Not only does the day go by more quickly, it flows and feels as if you're moving toward a destination. All types of jobs, regardless of surface differences, take on more life, love, and meaning. While there are instances when More means changing jobs or even careers, the More allows you to transform your current work, no matter what it is. The transformation is in you, not your workplace. By focusing on the More, you will advance and move to satisfaction with much less effort.

Jack, for instance, was a public defender in a large city who engaged heavily in the mood soft addiction of cynicism. Jack retreated to his cynical shell when he felt stressed, a common condition in the public defender's office. Just a few years removed from his law school idealism, Jack walked around grousing constantly about his job, his clients, and his bosses. Deeply enmeshed in all the petty irritations that came with his position, Jack was sure he needed to switch jobs.

Through living with More, Jack learned to recognize his deeper feelings, acknowledge his longing to make a difference, and notice his fear that his efforts were futile. He found renewed meaning in his service and cared more deeply for most of his clients. As he managed his cynical soft addiction (as well as some other addictions), he started seeing his clients as people again rather than "lost causes." Though some of them were guilty of crimes, most had redeeming qualities, and some were clearly innocent. Jack found himself energized by most cases. Win or lose, he found he could help most of his clients in some way. He generally resisted the impulse to be cynical and even became a bit of a crusader. Each day presented many new opportunities for Jack to help others, and he felt blessed and thankful for the opportunity.

What Is More at Home?

You may be worn out from work or from taking care of the kids, but focusing on the More causes you to consciously face your emotions and thereby feel more alive, even when you are tired at the end of a hard day. Boredom is a thing of the past as you reach out to others for contact, support, and reassurance. Life at home becomes a rich source of conscious, emotional experience. Instead of reading escapist fiction with no emotional resonance, you are more likely to find yourself laughing with a neighbor over the children's antics or sobbing with a friend over a loss. Your humor and spontaneity are more available because you are not avoiding painful truths. When alone, you find more meaning as you are dazzled by a misty morning walk or moments of prayer, contemplation, or reflection. Being at home becomes a much more sensual experience. Meaning can be found in little things—a deliciously baked cookie, a rest on the hammock when the sky is colored a brilliant pink, or a deeply felt conversation with a spouse or significant other. A day doesn't pass without something meaningful and life-affirming happening. You discover new riches daily, no matter if you live in the most beautiful area of the country or in an urban apartment.

Joan, a student at the Institute, started bringing More into her life after going on a pilgrimage with me to southern France. Raised in a family with few spiritual leanings, Joan grew up in a somber household that emphasized functionality over fun and utility over beauty. Going on pilgrimage opened Joan's eyes and heart to a different way of living. The closeness of the pilgrims' community modeled a kind of warmth and interaction that Joan realized she wanted for her family. She also experienced the power of prayer on pilgrimage, and began incorporating that into her life, too.

Today, Joan enjoys an important job with a big corporation and all the hustle and responsibility that brings. Yet she has learned to integrate her passion for work with a loving, vital home life that expresses her growing sense of beauty and spirituality.

Joan has left the austerity of her childhood behind. Her home is decorated with bright colors and comfy furniture that creates a vibrant and homey atmosphere her friends love to visit. Where once her children's music annoyed her, Joan now sings and even dances along with them. In the midst of all the bustle that's normal to family life, Joan still knows how to create a sense of calm and serenity around her, finding peace in her garden in the early morning, and in moments given to prayer.

Spirituality is now a touchstone for Joan. She says a prayer each day with her husband. She carries a deeper sense of the divine with her everywhere she goes, which informs her work as a manager, her leadership as a mother and wife, and her gifts of time and support to her community. Folks who know Joan count her a blessing in their lives, for she has learned how to give and take, to serve and to guide, living toward More all her days.

What Is More in Relationships?

Relationships with More make you feel connected deeply to another person—not just romantically but in all types of relationships. Many of us go through life forming pleasant, superficial acquaintances that we call "friendships." They are flimsy things that lack the glue of emotion and open communication. When you have More in relationships, you don't necessarily increase the quantity of these relationships but the quality grows. Imagine enjoying both robust laughter and wordless understanding with others, tenderly being able to sense their moods and joke about what's on your minds. There is no holding back in these relationships, no fear of how the other person might react to what you say. The bonds are deep and resilient, with enough space for the full range of emotions. A few words will not break them.

More means deriving far more pleasure (and sometimes pain) from interaction with others than is possible in superficial relationships. Interactions are electric with meaning and possibilities. You leave the time spent with these people feeling challenged and fulfilled.

Alex had a million friends, but he gradually learned that the friendships were only temporary, based on shared interests, shared soft addictions, and work. Gregarious, handsome, and highly successful, Alex collected people like shells at the beach. When he'd first meet someone, they'd do many things together, but over time they'd burn each other out and he'd go on to the next person. Sometimes he'd call up the old person, often to invite him or her to a party, but the relationship was always on the surface.

After learning to manage a number of soft addictions—especially the buzz of parties and gossip—Alex found he derived much more pleasure from deeper friendships. He met Gerald, an information technology specialist, when he purchased a new data management package. Gerald was almost the opposite of Alex: quiet, not particularly attractive or social, and immersed in his work. But Gerald and Alex found they could communicate with each other in emotional, highly personal ways thanks to Alex's new discoveries of More. Alex had just broken up with his girlfriend, and it seemed like Gerald understood the pain he was going through with an uncanny kind of empathy. Over time, Gerald and Alex became best friends, relishing how they could communicate with each other on both emotional and intellectual levels. This was but one of the wonders Alex discovered when he began to ask More of his relationships.

What Is More in Spirituality?

Having more spirituality in your life can translate into 1,001 things. Spirituality could be a connection with God or the universe, or finding yourself transported and transformed by prayer. It can mean being infused every day with a new sense of reverence for all you see. When you bring More spirituality into your life, you leave the distinction between the spiritual and the mundane behind. You find spiritual challenges and development in every moment of your life, be they moments of joy and peace or turmoil and heartache. More spirituality means you have a much fuller sense of who you are and your place on this earth. You don't wander around in a haze thinking, "Why was I born?" You gain the great satisfaction of knowing that your existence is meaningfully woven into the constantly unfolding tapestry of life. Spirituality is often thought of as a mysterious, ephemeral thing, but living the More generates a sense of rootedness. It brings the practicality of spirituality to light with the belief that each moment you live connects you to a greater purpose.

Emily used to anxiously bite her nails and constantly worry about the tiniest problems. Her ability to live with More spirituality blossomed as she reduced her mood addictions. Ironically, the blossoming began with the fear and sadness that followed her father's heart attack. Out of the five children, Emily was most like him. She figured her worries were leading her to the same type of health crisis. She began to change by taking yoga and learning meditation. It was not until she attended a soft addictions workshop with me that she recognized her unconscious belief in a punishing rather than a loving God.

Following the workshop, Emily realized she could bring more spirituality into her life by examining her limiting beliefs in an uncaring, dangerous world. She began challenging this belief by engaging in assignments that helped her see herself as the child of a loving, caring universe. She risked sharing judgments with others, made mistakes on purpose, and acted silly—all behaviors she would have avoided in the past. She was shocked to discover the goodwill of others in situations where she expected to be put down and rejected. She began to believe more and more in a loving universe. She focused on connecting with spirit through practices such as prayer and pilgrimage as well as spending time reflecting about her life on daily walks along the lake.

Her work transformed from martyrdom to adventure. Her relationships felt safe and loving, even in the face of increased truth and honesty. Though she still worried about things, she no longer worried intensely or constantly. Her prayers relieved her stomach-knotting agony. She found it much more satisfying to talk and pray about a problem rather than worry it to death. Her walks gave her time to digest her action-packed days and think calmly and deeply about the challenges in her life. She even developed a sense that she was being lovingly watched over, as if there were a benign force in the world that looked out for her. Everyone told Emily she seemed happier and calmer. Some wondered what she had "done." What they all saw was the reflection of the More in Emily's renewed spiritual connection.

What Is More in a Crisis?

Pursuing the More not only helps you develop a more satisfying life, it also prepares you to deal with difficult situations and crises. By becoming more conscious and more able to deal with your emotions, you respond to life's challenges more productively. You see meaning and opportunity in all that you experience.

For example, two days after the tragedy of September 11, 2001, I met with students in an ongoing More group I lead. Their presence and awareness moved me, as did the leadership they provided for their families, businesses, and communities. They said their training in consciousness helped them to focus on what really mattered and to respond compassionately and effectively rather than go numb. Instead of trapping themselves in a glazed haze in front of the TV or engaging in circular gossip, they felt their feelings. They faced their pain, their shock, and their fear. They cried big tears. And they expressed their outrage and anger. They rallied their families and gathered coworkers and community members for discussion groups, prayer vigils, and volunteer work. Knowing that overexposure to the television would be deadening, they chose to watch television judiciously for new information rather than repeated coverage. They recognized how important it was to be with people, to acknowledge and share their feelings, and to be thoughtful in their responses and wise in their actions. They served as points of contact and sources of rational thinking. Not paralyzed with fear, they were very present and alive and making a difference.

The process of achieving More is designed to fulfill spiritual hungers, and stopping our soft addictions is the specific challenge we face on our way to living the More. When you feed that deeper hunger, soft addictions naturally wane. At the same time, when you set your sights on the real More, you lose interest in the routine behaviors and moods that once seemed so important.

Creating More doesn't just happen by labeling or defining it. Your wish for More will inspire the actions required to fulfill that wish. The skills you will learn in the following chapters will help you further define your More and learn how to live it. The first step is to make the One Decision.

3.

MAKING THE ONE DECISION: TO BE OR NOT TO BE

"We must make choices that enable us to fulfill
the deepest capacities of our real selves."

—THOMAS MERTON

The One Decision is your commitment to living a life of
More. We all face the decision between living deep, conscious lives, or shallow, unconscious ones. We need to commit to one way of living versus another. This is not just *a*
decision. It is the One Decision that determines the quality
and direction of our life.

Making the One Decision may be the most important
decision you make in your life. It has the potential to influ-
ence every aspect of your life in positive ways. Yet, if you're
like most people, you probably don't realize that the decision is yours to make. We often go through life thinking,
This is just the way it is. It seems the best we can do is get by.
We numb ourselves to the pain with soft addictions and just
cope with the grind. Without the One Decision, we floun-
der. At times, we may realize that something isn't right and
try to do something about it, but the nagging feeling lingers:
There must be more than this. We haven't yet discovered the
power of making the One Decision that leads to a life of
More.

Making the One Decision is a commitment, the commitment to a life of More and to the steps that you'll take on the road to More. You have yet to formally identify your soft addictions, develop a vision of what a life of More looks like, and learn the skills of the process, but even now you stand at the edge of the great excitement and fulfillment that comes with making the One Decision. In making this decision and learning to live it, many of you will be learning about the very nature of commitment. You may be excited or afraid. But if you hunger for More—if you're fed up with your routines and what feels like a superficial existence—then you possess the drive and the desire to make this commitment, a commitment that will guide you through the steps of this book as well as your life.

THE UNDECISION VS. THE ONE DECISION

For a time in my life, I resigned myself to accepting that the best I could hope for was good career progress supplemented by distractions, escapes, and soft addictions. I indulged in overeating and looked out for newer and better ways to escape and zone out. I was overweight, overwrought, and underliving. I then made what I thought was an important decision. I decided to lose weight, and I did that.

I lost weight, but my life was still heavily involved with the soft addiction of food—what I wasn't going to eat, what I would eat, when I was going to eat, how much I was going to eat. I became so skinny that my hipbones stuck out and were easily bruised. I read cookbooks and studied recipes as if they held the key to life.

What I hadn't done was decide to live a full, conscious, alive life. Sure, I looked alive, appearing on television and receiving national recognition for programs I developed, but this was superficial aliveness. Without making the One Decision, I lacked a key way to measure my other life choices. I was still missing a center to revolve around.

Only after I faced the unhappiness of my first marriage

did I start on the path of personal growth. I made my One Decision, determining that I was going to live consciously and pursue my real hungers. This was the first step on my journey to living a life of More.

By deciding to live an exceptional, conscious life, I committed to living a more considered life. I focused on winning much greater prizes than awards and losing weight. That meant I decided to be alive, feel my feelings, and face life fully. Once I made my One Decision, I kept my weight off with ease. It felt totally different. I found my eating patterns shifting and my food choices realigning. I enjoyed being in my body rather than seeing exercise as a necessary evil. I actively looked for and found ways to fulfill myself. My One Decision guided me. It gave me a reason to eat in moderation, since stuffing myself numbed me and I wanted to feel alive. I chose a multitude of ways to nourish myself emotionally, physically, and spiritually, and this led to an even more fulfilling career and a great marriage! It doesn't mean I attained perfection after making my One Decision. Being perfect isn't part of my One Decision; being responsible and growing in consciousness *are*.

LIFE LITE OR LIFE DEEP

In the broadest sense of the term, the One Decision is a choice between opposites: a deeply felt life or a barely felt one; meaningful activities or escapist activities; spirituality or superficiality. It means choosing between living in a pleasant, anesthetized haze or experiencing life in all its authentic pain and pleasure; between a vague self-awareness or an acute consciousness of our deepest feelings. It is choosing quality over quantity, spirit over matter. Making the One Decision is choosing to live a considered, conscious life, rather than just drifting in a fog. To be or not to be is the real decision, and whether or not we know it, it's one we make every day of our lives.

THE RIGHT STUFF WITH THE
WRONG DECISION

Many of us think we have chosen a deep or high-quality life, but actually we haven't. We may do some deep things or add some quality experiences, but we have not made an underlying decision that changes the fabric of our lives. I thought I was making an important decision when I decided to lose weight, but it wasn't the One Decision that would change my life. It was when I decided to live a conscious, deeply felt life that my life changed. Living this commitment is different from just adding conscious activities to your life.

More to do

Rent the movie *The Matrix* for a graphic illustration of a One Decision. The hero is given a choice of which pill to take—the one that shows him the full reality or the one that numbs him into a contrived, protected, unfeeling, consensual fantasy.

For example, I have friends who meditate for hours each day but continually complain and indulge in mood and other soft addictions. They still live frustrating, semi-satisfying lives, out of touch with their deeper wants. Adding a yoga class or in-depth courses in spiritual development isn't enough without the One Decision. However, with the One Decision, all the good things we do contribute to the larger whole and take us where we ultimately want to go.

Maya wanted to be perfect. To her, perfect meant being a particular weight, having a toned body, and making sure her hair looked just right. She began her regimen. She worked out, dieted, and consulted with her hairstylist on the perfect hair for her. She learned styling techniques and makeup application. One day while on vacation at Club Med, she awakened in the morning and thought, *This is it. This is the day. I am perfect. My weight is exactly right, my body is toned and tan, I'm having a great hair day.* But then she realized, *I have no one to tell. What do I do with this? Go down to the beach and say, 'Hey, I'm perfect today'? What's the point?*

A few years later, Maya is still in great shape, but she defines it differently. She's made a different decision. It's her mind, body, and spirit that matter to her. She meditates, does Pilates, has a great relationship with a wonderful guy, and uses her business acumen and contacts to help others live More. She still experiences twinges of envy when she sees her friend who is a fashion model, but Maya knows it is her whole life that matters, not just being a perfect size 8. Her body is in shape, but now it is *her* shape, which is fit and healthy, but no longer "perfect."

THE POWER OF YOUR ONE DECISION

Your One Decision shines as a beacon. It beckons you and orients you through times of confusion. The One Decision guides living in ideal situations but also guides decisions in difficult times. It gives us a sense of direction and control in times when we don't feel like we have much control. We can always align to a higher principle or value. We can always choose how we want to experience something and how we respond.

When you make your One Decision, you choose to pursue the greater More of life. Your One Decision also sustains you throughout the rest of the process. You'll be ready to identify and release your soft addictions because they hinder your path to a conscious life.

How might your life change were you to decide to live more deeply and consciously every day, recognizing your spiritual hungers and aligning your thoughts and activities to fulfill them? What if all you do fits into a more meaningful whole? Imagine never thinking, *There must be more than this*, because you had found the More. Picture yourself at the end of a typical day feeling energized and sensitized to every aspect of your world.

To be this way requires a decision. Of course, choosing

our soft addictions constitutes a de facto decision. We usually aren't conscious of this decision and its implications; we don't understand that we've opted for a numb existence instead of a fully alive one. At times, though, the numbness wears off and we glimpse the terrible possibility that we are wasting our lives.

In our glazed, softly addicted state, we aren't sufficiently aware to grasp the decision before us. Our soft addictions steal our aliveness and short-circuit our soul's longing. As a result, we infrequently reach the point where we ask, *What do I want to say about myself at the end of my life?* Who would want to answer, *I spent a gazillion hours online, daydreaming, and trying to make more money than I did the year before.* Blinded by our soft addictions, we don't see that we can choose to ask, *Have I lived a deep and meaningful life, defined by my desire to be closer to myself, to others, to nature, and to God?*

The One Decision demands rigor, requiring soul-searching and commitment. We need to make it if we plan on taking the next steps. We can proclaim today we will live a highly spiritual, authentic life and tomorrow go back on that decision. If you treat the One Decision like a New Year's resolution, you'll soon slip back into your soft addiction routines.

September 11, 2001, jarred many people into awareness of what was most important to them. With this awareness, many made a type of One Decision that changed their lives. Most, however, shifted for a while, but returned to their older patterns. They had a sudden awareness but didn't make the underlying life-altering decision. I'd like to help you make a decision that you'll stick with and that you'll embrace with every fiber of your being. At the end of this chapter, you'll be able to make a One Decision that will endure and guide you for the rest of your life.

COMMON CHOICES

Making the One Decision translates into many personal choices. If you decide to live a soulful life, it follows that you will change the way you spend your time and energy. For one person, this might mean spending less time mindlessly shopping and more time talking mindfully to close friends. For another, it might mean quitting a boring, unfulfilling job and pursuing your life's work. Obviously, the One Decision has implications that vary from individual to individual.

But not every decision is on that scale. Each day, we make hundreds, if not thousands, of decisions. From what to wear to what to think about in our idle moments to what we're going to do for lunch, we are steeped in choices. All day long we make decisions without a real guiding philosophy. We are often confused by all our options or we fall into routines that make our choices automatically. Our One Decision can provide guidance, a yardstick with which we can measure all things.

Consciously making the One Decision saves us from thousands of ill-considered decisions and endless internal debate, bargaining, and mind chatter. We more easily see which activity or mood leads to a deeper relationship with ourselves, to higher consciousness, or even to God. People

> More-sel
>
> "You don't get to choose how you're going to die. Or when. You can only decide how you're going to live. Now."
>
> —JOAN BAEZ

> More-sel
>
> "Living is a constant process of deciding what we are going to do."
>
> —JOSÉ ORTEGA Y GASSET

who are constantly agonizing about what to do or who let their routines decide for them have not made the One Decision.

The following are common decisions. Note which option out of each pair you would be more likely to choose. For now, pick realistically, not idealistically.

A. Flipping through the channels just trying to chill out and distract yourself until it's time for bed.

B. Searching the television guide for a program that addresses a topic or issue that you care about or that's related to a significant problem or event taking place in your life.

A. Sleeping a little late and then rushing off to work.

B. Getting up a little early to journal and get in touch with yourself.

A. Talking with a friend about who's going out with whom.

B. Talking with a friend about what's going on inside of you.

A. Spending a weekend day continuously shopping, cleaning the house, and doing other chores straight through from morning to night.

B. Taking a break from weekend chores and spending time just by yourself in nature, listening to music or a thoughtful radio program, or meditating.

A. Consistently working six or seven days a week and complaining bitterly about "the stupid job."

B. Recognizing that your attitude is grinding down your soul and beginning a search for a more rewarding career.

A. Choosing to spend unnecessary time at work rather than participate in family activities.

B. Doing what you need to do at work so you have time to be with your family.

A. Gobbling fast food from plastic containers while watching hours of mediocre situation comedies.

B. Setting the table, playing great music, lighting a candle, and inviting yourself to dinner.

A. Fantasizing in idle hours at work or at home about material things or relationships with people you barely know.

B. Being proactive and highly conscious about doing things that will satisfy your spiritual hungers.

All of us, whether or not we've made the One Decision, choose A over B at times. If, however, you fill your life with A responses and other soft addictions, you need to break free. Breaking free is a process you will learn in the following chapters. The first step is to make your One Decision. Once you've made it, you'll find yourself gravitating more to B than A responses. It's as if that decision adjusts your life compass, providing you with a stronger sense of direction in a world of confusing choices.

WHAT DOES A ONE DECISION LOOK LIKE?

The expression of the One Decision is personal and unique. Later in this chapter, I'm going to ask you to articulate your One Decision. With that challenge in mind, look at how two people expressed their decisions:

I have decided. I have made the One Decision. I have decided to live an exceptional life, a conscious life, to fulfill my spiritual hungers, to live deeply, to feel deeply, to open myself to all life has to offer and to greet it. I have decided to be open to my pain, to feel my feelings, to let them wash across my face. A life worth liv-

ing is one that is felt deeply, where all experiences are worthy of being experienced. I need not numb myself. I can take it. I invite it. I choose life!

I commit. I am a force to be reckoned with. This is my most trusted ally and I choose truth. My gifts are to be shared. I will not hide. I am an active player in life, committed to aliveness. With intention and energy, I pursue love and connection. I am deeply committed to manifesting spirit in everything I do. I will do anything to further peace in my heart. I will work tirelessly to bring together the sides of me that are at war. No stone will be left unturned, no opportunity left untried. There is no boundary I fear to cross. I will have it all. My One Decision is made.

These are two very different expressions of the same decision: to lead a life of More. What unites the two expressions is the recognition of our yearnings for the divine or something greater than ourselves, for love, acceptance, and peace. They express elements of More—more life, love, meaning, feelings, consciousness, energy, and other aspects. They lead to the recognition of people as worthy and magnificent who deserve exceptional lives. Tremendously powerful touchstones, their "authors" can always come back to their decisions when in doubt or distress. No matter what type of problem or opportunity, they can always refer to the One Decision. If they're feeling down, it can inspire; when they're unsure, it points toward a course of action. It provides momentum and guidance as they climb the steps necessary to rise above their soft addictions.

Making the One Decision, however, doesn't mean that you will never indulge in your soft addictions again. That isn't the point. But the next time you find yourself mindlessly channel surfing or engaging in hours of gossiping, you will have a way of managing the soft addiction. Your consciousness of your actions will intrude: You'll recall the One Decision that you made, and it will help you limit the time and energy that you devote to these empty pursuits.

The One Decision helps you be with yourself in a new way. It allows you to ask yourself more interesting questions when you're engaged in a soft addiction. For instance, you'll ask yourself, *Why am I spending all this time in front of the television? Is it helping me get in touch with my deeper yearnings? Does watching* Friends *add more meaning and resonance to my life than being with my own friends?* Instead of chastising yourself for watching so much television, making an excuse to justify your habit (*I've had a tough day; I deserve this*), or just zoning out and not thinking at all, you can refer to your One Decision and address your soft addiction differently. The One Decision to live a considered life helps you discover the "Why" underneath your soft addiction routines. Whether you have that One Decision in your mind or on a piece of paper, you can refer to it, view your activities or moods in a new light, and gain the strength and motivation to move toward more meaningful endeavors.

To illustrate the impact of the One Decision, let's take the example of two people, Laura and Jeff, who are preparing for a big meeting at work. From the moment Jeff wakes up, he's a nervous wreck. Everything seems to go wrong. He couldn't sleep well because of anxiety about the meeting. Exhausted, he slept through his alarm and rushed to get to the office. Jeff barely spoke to his wife and children as he flew around the house getting ready, gulping coffee to be alert. He drove, frenzied, to the office, speed-weaving through traffic while constantly pushing the radio buttons to distract himself.

Laura, on the other hand, woke up anxious about the meeting, but her One Decision to be in touch with her emotions and to value herself and her loved ones allows her to make a series of choices that immediately calm her. She begins her morning by accepting her feelings and meditating about them, sitting in a special place in her house where she knows she will be undisturbed. Refreshed from her meditation, Laura wakes her husband and gives him a hug, feeling cared for and valued by his return embrace. Though her husband is responsible for waking their children and getting them ready for school this week, she goes into each of their rooms and kisses them and says good-bye. She has left herself time to review the presentation. On the way to work, she listens to a CD she loves and is grateful for all the roles she is allowed to play.

The One Decision put all of Laura's other decisions into perspective. Jeff lacked a perspective-creating device and so he alternately fled from and was stirred up by his feelings.

DECIDING TO GO ON A JOURNEY

I don't want to give the false impression that the One Decision is a panacea. Deciding is simply the start of the journey and along the way missteps occur.

Kendra, a student at the Wright Institute, was in the grip of many soft addictions, one of them being coffee. Now this might seem like an innocuous habit, but in fact, not only was Kendra spending a lot of money on her habit (she estimated over $2,500 annually), but it made her feel anxious and jittery. She liked the buzz it gave her, the ritual of going to Starbucks, and the familiar role of coffee drinker—it was reassuring to repeat the same behaviors daily and give herself a break.

After making her One Decision to fully experience her life, Kendra stepped back from this coffee ritual. She decided she wanted to really feel alive, not just accept the caffeine buzz she substituted for aliveness. She then found that coffee was no longer as satisfying, that she needed activities and positive moods to help her feel more alive and vital. As a result, she began learning to dance, finding that grace and movement conferred a sense of freedom. Kendra also started going for walks in the woods and began to feel more a part of the natural world around her. She unleashed her creativity by writing short stories, designing and making quilts, and adding decorative touches to her home.

Kendra's journey has not been perfectly smooth. She talks about the stupid things she still does when she wants to impress a guy or how her procrastination is a soft addiction she clings to. She even indulges in a three-dollar cup of coffee now and then. Kendra, though, is intensely alert to these addictions as well as the activities that bring her authenticity and meaning. The One Decision woke her up. She consciously notices things in her life rather than sleepwalking through it. Existing, for Kendra, is much more intense and feeling-focused. She feels she's going somewhere now that her life has a destination.

People ask me what it's like after you resolve to live a highly conscious life; how it feels to have made the One Decision. I refer to others who have provided me with feedback. They describe how their vision goes from blurry to clear; how life becomes an adventure; how they start to feel More; and how they become more in tune with the world.

Most of all, people talk about starting on a journey, opening a new door onto a fresh path. While you may have miles to go before you become spiritually fulfilled or find the meaning in life you're seeking, you experience a strong feeling of moving in a new direction. The journey becomes fulfilling in itself. The excitement and energy of the path facilitate taking the next steps.

WHY YOU DON'T NEED TO BECOME MOTHER TERESA OR GANDHI

Perhaps the One Decision sounds ominous, as if you're making a reverse Faustian pact, an agreement with an angel rather than the devil. While it is a momentous decision, it's not a black or white one. Making it doesn't mean that you must live a purely spiritual life or that you can no longer indulge in any soft addictions. It is nothing more—and nothing less—than a shift in how you see the world. Don't expect to be transformed into a saint or a monk, but expect changes to occur. Here are the ones that most people experience:

Asking the big questions. You will stop asking the small questions and start asking the big ones. The typical small questions include: "What should I wear?" "What gadget should I buy?" "What dessert do I want?" We expend tremendous amounts of time and energy on these little questions, most of which relate to surface issues. While it's fine to occasionally look for a nice dress, it's not fine to agonize for weeks over what dress to buy for a party and waste hours going from one store to another.

After making the One Decision, people will still ask these small questions and they will still pick out a dress to wear or a gadget to buy. But the decision is more integrated, and the dress is more likely to reflect who they really are, and the gadget is more likely to have a higher purpose than to just have the latest and coolest thing. The small questions will transform into inquiries like: "Which choice helps me move toward my vision?" More important, they will start asking the Big Questions and spend time contemplating the answers. Big Questions include: "What is my purpose and what helps me fulfill it?" "Why am I here and how do I make my life count?" and "What gives my life meaning?"

Experiencing more intense feelings. You will experience more intense feelings. The numbness recedes once we make the One Decision. The joyfulness, energy, and even euphoria are part of an emotional rush that comes after deciding. At the same time, asking the Big Questions also makes us feel fear and sadness. Exploring your purpose can be a struggle, and you may have to confront years of wastefulness in which you acted without purpose. Be prepared to laugh with great joy and cry with great sorrow; you cannot experience one without the other.

Reframing addictive behaviors. You will reframe your soft addictions. By "reframe," I mean a gradual change in your perspective on your soft addictions. You'll start viewing every mood and activity through your One Decision. You won't eat, smoke, work out, gossip, or daydream without thinking, *What am I feeling now? What is going on with me that I want to do this now? How will this lead me to knowledge about myself, to more awareness and more sustenance?* As a result, you'll reframe television watching as a window to worlds you wouldn't ordinarily experience. Instead of surfing the Net in a mindless daze, you'll use it to focus on a specific inquiry designed to satisfy a deeper need. Instead of reading to escape, you'll read for knowledge, inspiration, and wisdom.

You'll begin to examine your motivations for doing what you do and feeling what you feel. This examination allows you to be less dependent on your soft addictions. Or more accurately, you change soft addictions into meaningful behaviors.

Here's a perfect example of how the One Decision refocuses and reframes. As I was writing the previous paragraph, I started to feel anxious and noticed a clutch in my gut concerning an engagement tonight. I reflexively felt the urge to check out: to take a nap, to grab a cup of coffee, to make some chorelike phone calls, and so on. But the One Decision helped me become aware of this reflex. My decision to be conscious and in touch with my feelings led me to identify my anxiety and to see how I was responding. I knew to look beneath my urges for my soft addictions to discover what I'm feeling. Rather than checking out, I took a meaningful break. I listened to a favorite song and made a cup of great tea and got in touch with my feelings. I closed my eyes for a moment, reviewing and adjusting my plans for the evening until I felt satisfied. I felt the tension release. Doing so relaxed me and allowed me to return to this writing, refreshed and aware that this was something important to me. There's a big difference between consciously choosing breaks and checking out.

ARTICULATING YOUR ONE DECISION

You have moved toward your One Decision by picking up this book and reading to this point. Now it is time to affirm your commitment. Some people discover that they can naturally engage in reflection and find memorable and moving words to make their One Decision. Many others, however, find that the following steps facilitate the articulation of their One Decision:

1. *Reflect on your reasons.* Find a quiet, peaceful spot and reflect upon why you want to make the One Decision. Consider what's prompting you to make this decision. Why do you want More in your life? Are you unhappy? Are there times when you feel empty and unconnected? Are you unable to experience great joy, backing away from even positive, strong feelings? Do you have yearnings that you want to fulfill? What excites you about a different type of life? Write down what's prompting you to make the decision.

2. *Identify your wants.* What do you want More of in your life? Review the definitions of More in the last chapter— more life, love, meaning, feelings, consciousness, energy, satisfaction, purpose, flow, resources, etc., as well as any other words you would use to describe the More. Which aspects do you want More of in your life? What do you hunger for deep in your heart? What would make your life a well-lived life? What do you want to be able to say about your life at the end of your life? Proclaim what you want More of in your life by writing it down.

3. *Claim your commitment.* Claim your life of More by writing your personal commitment. Compose a paragraph expressing your One Decision. Use the previous two exercises as raw material. You may want to refer back to the examples of the One Decision in this chapter. Be reinspired by the More-sel quote by Jack London earlier in this chapter.

Enjoy playing with possibilities. Write your decision in the affirmative, not as a wish or by saying "I want to." Create a living statement that can grow with you and become more clear as your One Decision comes into greater focus throughout your life. Remember, the decision is final, but the wording and understanding may vary over time. You are deciding to live a life of More.

Your One Decision recognizes your yearning and hunger for the divine, for love, acceptance, aliveness, or peace. It is a decision that will lead you to recognize that you are a worthy, magnificent person who deserves a life of More.

After you've written your One Decision, recite it. Feel the words you've written and express them passionately. You may also find it helps to say them to another individual who you believe will appreciate the One Decision you're making. What you're asking this other person to do is witness your One Decision. Once you've expressed your One Decision, keep it with you at all times. Even if you've memorized it, make the actual words a permanent part of you by carrying them with you or by placing them in a special place in your home.

Your One Decision is now a beacon to guide you and a foundation to support you as you learn to live the life of More you have chosen. With your One Decision in mind, you're now ready to move forward and identify the soft addictions that have been part of your life for such a long time.

4.

IDENTIFYING YOUR
SOFT ADDICTIONS

*"I generally avoid temptation unless
I can't resist it."*

—MAE WEST

Without fail, in the twelve years since we coined "soft addictions," people respond with an "Aha!" when they first hear the term. They immediately identify a common soft addiction or even mention an addiction of their own: "Oh, yeah, like watching too much television," or "I spend a lot of time on the Internet." After they learn more, they generally discover even more soft addictions, such as gossiping, nail biting, or collecting things. Then there are always those who are more eloquent about the soft addictions of others: "My husband is a sports fanatic," or "My wife is into shoes."

Most of us can identify at least one activity that hooks us. It's the rare person who doesn't admit to being addicted to television, sports, shopping, work, or any of the typical leisure-time endeavors. What's more difficult is identifying the less apparent soft addiction routines that have us in their grip. They're not always as obvious as television and they're often far more insidious. We're not used to thinking about moods as something that we might be addicted to, unaware of how we can use familiar moods as a refuge. Similarly, many people are addicted to avoidance patterns, such as procrastination or steering clear of social interactions.

In addition, we enmesh ourselves in scores of "smaller" routines, ones that may seem innocuous on the surface but whose cumulative impact is significant. We spend enormous amounts of unproductive time on these little things—from compulsive e-mail checking to nail picking to overgrooming (combing hair, putting on makeup, etc.) to getting weather updates ten times a day.

As harmless as they may appear, these activities deprive us of time and energy that could be devoted to more meaningful pursuits. We may not realize that our drive to constantly check the status of our investments qualifies as a soft addiction, but it's one of many little habits that keep us trapped in a world of Less.

Denial and defensiveness compound the difficulty of identifying our addictions. We'll focus on this problem in greater detail in the next chapter. For now you should be aware that you most likely deny, rationalize, or make excuses for at least some of your soft addiction routines. The odds are that you've developed credible explanations to yourself about why these routines are not addictions or not a problem. It's also possible that you admit these soft addictions are a problem but not one of sufficient magnitude to worry about. Instead, you ascribe your addictive behaviors to "being human" and suggest that everyone has a "weakness." Thus, you have trouble identifying your soft addictions because you view them as minor flaws rather than as obstacles to getting More out of life.

Certainly making the One Decision helps us see our addictive behaviors and moods for what they really are. When

2. Francine Hardaway, "Under the Radar: Television 2.0," *BizAz*, vol. 5 (July/August 2002), p. 80.

we decide to live life deeply, it's easier to recognize a superficial behavior. With the greater consciousness that the One Decision confers, we are better equipped to spot these addictions. Even so, soft addictions often elude well-trained eyes, as the following story illustrates.

THERE'S MORE THAN MEETS THE EYE

Jason was well aware that he wasted enormous amounts of time on the Internet, both at work and at home. He freely admitted he was hooked on gaming, sports, and sex-related sites. Not only did his wife complain about the amount of time he spent in front of the computer, but he had also been reprimanded more than once at work for personal Internet surfing. Jason made token efforts to cut back on his Internet activity and recognized it as a type of addiction.

What he didn't recognize was that this big addiction masked scores of smaller and more amorphous ones. For instance, every day he snacked on candy bar after candy bar and almost every night he went to the gym and played basketball with the guys because he felt guilty about eating so much candy. Jason was a bit overweight and hated the extra pounds. To him, the snacking and exercising canceled each other out and he viewed both activities as part of his "lifestyle" rather than a life-numbing routine.

Jason didn't grasp that his addictions existed on another level. When he wasn't online, he got his buzz from the fantasies in his head. Some of them were sexual; others revolved around escape fantasies and vengeance. He felt that his bosses picked on him and he imagined scenarios in which he exacted retribution for their unfair treatment of him. In addition, Jason was also addicted to acting aloof. His demeanor at home and especially at work was that of a stoic, never letting anyone see him upset (or joyous, for that matter). In Jason's mind, this "cool" persona was who he wanted to be. It made him feel like an actor in an action movie who was completely in control. Of course, the routines were really controlling Jason. He was stuck in a superficial existence. Once he made the One Decision, he started to see his behaviors and moods for what they were. When Jason started to identify his various soft addictions, he was amazed not only at their number but also at how they all seemed linked—from his overeating to his compulsive working out to his movie watching to his stoic demeanor.

Identifying soft addictions takes a bit of practice, but once you start doing it, you become perceptive about the linkages between various moods and behaviors. You realize that soft addictions may exist in all shapes and sizes, but they all serve the same purpose: they numb you to your feelings and your deeper, spiritual self.

It's often easier to identify the soft addictions in others. As an exercise, think of someone you know well. Start out listing the more common soft addictions they may have (television, gossiping, working out). Then list the smaller or idiosyncratic ones (coupon clipping, collecting salt and pepper shakers, hair twirling, etc.). Do they also have addictions related to moods, things, and avoidances? If you're having trouble, make a preliminary list of what that person did in the last week—how he or she spent his or her time. By listing activities that took up big chunks of time, you'll gain insights about what his or her soft addictions are. While it's more difficult to identify another's mood addictions, you may be able to venture a good guess based on themes in conversations with that person. For instance, someone who tells you that he or she spends hours dreaming about a television actor or who complains about always feeling "blah" is telling you what activities and moods he or she gravitates toward.

CHANGING OUR PERCEPTIONS OF SOFT ADDICTIONS

Identifying our soft addictions is impossible if we resist categorizing them as addictions. Admittedly, "addiction" is a problematic word. For many people, the word denotes skid-row bums, needles, drunken binges, and the like. Even though most experts recognize that hard addictions represent a disease, there still remains the too widely held view that they are the result of a weak will or a moral flaw.

As a result, people don't like to admit that they're addicted to anything, be it soft or hard. What we need to come to terms with is the ubiquitous nature of addictions and how the addictive process runs through everyone's life. We all give ourselves over to things. In fact, the word "addiction" comes to us from Roman law, meaning "to give over." Our society has accumulated a great deal of wisdom and information in treating hard addictions, and we can apply some of that knowledge to soft addictions. The desperate need to escape, the comfortably familiar routines, and the numbing of feelings are integral to both hard and soft addictions. By getting past our aversion to this word, we can place our counterproductive behaviors in context. Once we see we're addicted, or have surrendered or dedicated ourselves to addictive behaviors, we can start learning how to manage the addiction.

Consider the following list of excuses and rationalizations we fall back on when confronted with our soft addictions:

"After working hard, I need to escape."
"It's just harmless fun."
"This is just my hobby."
"Everyone does this."
"I wouldn't know what to do if I couldn't do this."
"This is part of who I am."
"All my friends do the same things, so what would
we do if we didn't do this?"

Identification of soft addictions is terribly difficult if you make these excuses and rationalizations. It's natural to react defensively when someone points out your soft addiction; you feel guilty to be wasting so much time on a particular behavior. In a larger sense, however, there is nothing to feel guilty about: we all have our soft addictions. In their most benign form, soft addictions are harmless hobbies and necessary escapes from stress. To eliminate them entirely is difficult if not impossible. On the other hand, they cease to be harmless or merely an escape when they prevent us from getting More out of life. Then they are a problem and need to be identified.

Tyrone, for instance, is a personal trainer who initially defended his six-days-a-week, two-and-a-half-hour physical fitness routine as a "healthy" activity and one that fit his nature. Tyrone admitted that he can't sit still, becoming antsy just sitting through a movie. As a result, he chose a profession that allows him to be in almost constant motion. Even when he isn't doing his job or working out, he gravitates from one physical challenge to another.

Despite his ability to meet his need for motion, Tyrone did not feel particularly happy or satisfied. He reported using exercise to "fight off anxiety," and he became agitated just thinking about having to sit and do nothing. He mistakenly believed that his More resided in increasing his level of exercise—that somehow he could satisfy his spiritual hunger if he just ran, lifted, and rode more.

Tyrone worked on how to relax through courses, learning laboratories, and individual coaching at the Institute for months before he could admit that exercise was a way for him to run from feelings. In several of his classes, Tyrone worked on exercises and assignments designed to facilitate emotional expression. He was shocked at how his tears flowed, how his anger exploded in these exercises. During the week, between classes, he found himself more relaxed and joyful. To his surprise and delight, he discovered that he

> ## More to think about
>
> How might you defend your routines to a friend or loved one? How might you explain or justify your addictive behaviors? Would you act resentful at being accused of having an addiction?

could express his feelings easily and spontaneously. He felt liberated when he acknowldged that he used workouts to escape. This acknowledgment started him on a path to letting more of himself—his authentic self—surface.

While Tyrone continued his job (which he loved), he weaned himself from reflex exercising and became comfortable with the emotive and cerebral parts of himself. He entered a management training program that had previously intimidated him. As he became more genuine and at ease with his emotions, the quality of his relationships deepened. Currently he is dating a woman who appreciates both his competence and his expressiveness, and his life is more of an adventure than he'd ever imagined possible.

SEARCHING FOR RED FLAGS

Identifying addictions isn't a science. Some of your activities may fall on the cusp; others occupy a gray area where it's initially difficult to know with any certainty if they're soft addictions. For example, you may daydream at times (who doesn't?), but it's difficult to discern if your daydreaming is excessive or if it interferes with your ability to achieve your real dreams. It's also possible that you have a group of time wasters but your time commitment to each is relatively small—you don't do any of them to excess, making it difficult to detect their cumulative effect on the soft addiction radar.

More-sel

"Lead me not into temptation. I can find the way myself."

—RITA MAE BROWN

Therefore, at this point your goal shouldn't be to create a definitive list of every activity, mood, and avoidance in order of time consumed or energy zapped. Rather, use the following exercises to identify and attach red flags to parts of your life that clearly lead you in the wrong direction. Let them generate self-awareness about the moods and activities that rob your life of depth and richness.

TOOLS TO IDENTIFY YOUR SOFT ADDICTIONS

Review the list of soft addictions you first saw in Chapter 1, reprinted here, which is designed to get you thinking about soft addictions in terms of the four key categories or types of activities, moods, avoidances, and things. If you haven't done so already, go through each list and place a check mark next to the ones that might apply to you. Feel free to add any others you think of as you read the list. As you'll discover, some of the items listed may sound relatively unimportant (nail biting) compared with others (Web surfing or television watching). Remember, though, that a soft addiction doesn't have to be anything monumental to constitute a spiritual roadblock.

More to think about

How do you know if you have soft addictions? Check your pulse. If you feel it, be assured you have some. It's not whether you have soft addictions; it's which ones *do* you have.

Activities

Media

Watching television
    Channel surfing
    Program junkie
Surfing the Internet
Participating in chat rooms
Checking investments
Checking weather, statistics, news
Reading magazines
Reading only one genre of

novels, such as romance
    or mysteries
Listening to the radio
Checking e-mail
Playing computer games
Playing video games
Checking eBay

_____

_____

_____

Buying/Shopping

Shopping
Cruising garage sales
Collecting
Antiquing
Bargain hunting

Hanging out in the mall
Perusing catalogues
Clipping coupons
_____
_____

Maintenance

Overeating
Overexercising
Glamorizing
Hygiene
Housekeeping
Being a pack rat

Caregiving
Sleeping too much
Nail biting
_____
_____
_____

Physical Mannerisms

Hair twirling
Twitching, jiggling, picking
Gum chewing

_____
_____
_____

Sexual

Flirting
Sexual obsessions
Phone sex
Pornography
Masturbating compulsively
Being a voyeur

Babe or dude watching
Being promiscuous
Leering
Fantasizing
_____
_____

Work

Overworking/Keeping busy	_____
Overscheduling	_____
Overcommitting	_____

Risk Taking

Speeding	Making deals
Gambling	_____
Seeking danger	_____

Social/People

Name-dropping	Fantasizing/daydreaming
Following celebrity news	Lying
Gossiping	_____
Storytelling	_____

Other Diversions

Checking sports stats	_____
Doing crossword puzzles	_____
Playing card games	_____

Moods/Ways of Being

Being sarcastic	Being a drama king or
Being cranky/irritable	queen
Indulging in self-pity	Always being happy;
Being "in the know"	always "on"

Being a Pollyanna
Chameleonlike behavior
Acting like a sad sack
Moping
Blaming
Looking good
Complaining
Constantly trying to please
people

High energy
Jokester
Perfectionism
Fanaticism
Being argumentative/con-
flictual
Acting cool
_____
_____

Avoidances

Procrastinating
Isolating
Being late
Playing dumb
Living in clutter
Playing helpless
Playing the victim

Hypochondria
Phobias
Stonewalling
Being too busy
Oversleeping/napping
_____
_____

Things—edible and consumable

Sugar
Chocolate
Fast foods
Carbohydrates, high-fat
foods, etc.
Coffee
Snack foods
Cigarettes

Gadgets
Designer clothes
Collectibles
CDs
DVDs
Brand-name merchandise
_____
_____

SOFT ADDICTION QUIZ

If you're wondering if the items you checked are soft addictions, take this quiz. How many "yes" answers indicate that you have a soft addiction? Even a single "yes" answer might qualify! Use each one as a prompt to look deeper. Of course, the more "yes" answers you have, the more likely a given activity or mood qualifies as a soft addiction.

1. Would you be unlikely to go on national television and say "You, too, should do this" about your behavior?

2. When asked why you do this thing, do your reasons sound like an excuse or a rationalization?

3. Do you do this activity or retreat to a mood compulsively or habitually?

4. Is there a particular routine that you follow, almost like a ritual, for this behavior?

5. Do you have difficulty imagining life without it (or even with less of it)?

6. Do you want to change this behavior, resolve to do so, but then find yourself unable to keep your resolution?

7. Do you feel scared or stubborn when someone suggests you stop or reduce this behavior?

8. Has the time you spend doing the activity or being in the mood increased without providing the same level of satisfaction it once did?

9. Have you been teased, mocked, or criticized because of how you're wasting a great deal of your time on trivial pursuits?

10. Has someone close to you become annoyed or angry with you about the amount of time, money, and/or energy you devote to a given activity?

11. Have you canceled or turned down positive opportunities in order to indulge an activity, substance, or mood?

12. Has your particular activity, mood, or avoidance caused you to get in trouble on the job?

13. Is this something that you would be embarrassed about if others were to learn of it? Does it feel like a secret you're ashamed of?

After answering these questions, you'll probably have a better idea of what your top soft addictions are.

SOFT ADDICTION AWARENESS EXERCISES

If you are still unsure or would like to see how much of an issue your soft addictions are for you, use the following soft addiction–awareness exercises. (You can also find these and other tools on our Web site at *www.theremustbemore.com.*) As you identify your addictions, keep in mind that our concern is soft rather than hard addictions. This book is not designed to help individuals whose addictions are at clinically significant levels, such as people with eating disorders like anorexia or bulimia. In these instances, psychotherapy or counseling are appropriate resources.

How Much Time Do I Spend?

This is a simple but telling measure. Note approximately how much time you spend on each checked item during a given week. Make some guesses where you are uncertain, especially regarding moods and avoidances. The key is to give yourself a sense of whether you spend a lot, a middling, or just a little time on each activity or mood.

To further illuminate your time use, break them down into the following categories:

Doing: Time spent physically engaged in an activity.

Thinking: Time spent mentally engaged in an activity. This includes preparing for it (thinking about what you need in order to participate in it), fantasizing about it, and worrying about it.

Frequency: How often you engage in the behavior throughout a day or week.

As you look over the hours you've listed next to each item, do certain ones stand out because of the amount of time expended on them? Do you engage in some behaviors fairly frequently?

What Is My Motivation?

Beyond what you do and how much time you spend doing it, there's the issue of why you do it. Examining and understanding your motivation is critical. Two people can seem to be "zoned out." One, however, is in a semi-conscious state, stressed out, while another may be consciously meditating, focused intensely on contacting his inner self, oblivious to external stimulation. Similarly, some people listen to music for distraction, while others listen to be uplifted or educated. Or there's the difference between someone who shops to fill time, escape emotions, or because she can't resist a sale versus the individual who is looking for personally expressive or cost-effective clothes.

Look at each of the items you checked on the soft addictions list and determine your motivation for doing them. Is it high, low, or mid-

More to think about

A student at the Institute, a chief executive officer of a nationally recognized actuarial consulting company, calculated that he spent 1,000 hours a year worrying. This is an actuarial estimate by an expert—not a mere guess. Realizing that a full work-year is 2,000 hours, he now spends his time planning and talking things out instead of just worrying!

dle? High represents a spiritual or otherwise meaningful motivation, such as a desire to learn and grow. Low means your impulse is escapist, unconscious, unexamined, or aimed at fulfilling a surface need. Middle connotes an ambiguous or uncertain purpose.

As you examine your motivation for the checked items, pay attention to the ones that receive low marks because they are most likely to be soft addictions.

What Are My Feelings?

This last variable indicates how you feel around an activity or mood. Note how you feel at three points: before, during, and after the activity or mood. Focus on your checked items where you devote time and have low motivation. Be alert for the following words (or similar expressions of the same sentiments) because they often reflect the feelings of people in the grip of soft addictions:

Before

Anxious/jittery	Compulsive
Bored	Angry
Driven	Self-pitying
Sad	Afraid
Excited	

During

Zoned out	Buzzed
Numb	Getting high
Glazed	Increased agitation
Unconscious	

After

Embarrassed	Agitated
High	Buzzed
Shameful	Forgetful (can't remember
Glazed	what you've
Continued numbness	done/seen/heard)

If you find that you experience at least some of the feelings listed, you likely have a soft addiction. The most common soft addiction-induced feelings are the numbed, zoned-out state, or a kind of neutered emotion, such as a mildly pleasant buzz. This is a very different experience from a sense of joy or transcendence, states in which feelings are intensified rather than muted.

Growing in Awareness

These exercises are guides for you to become more self-aware and conscious of your habits. See what stands out for you. What feels surprising or even alarming when you note its frequency or the accompanying feelings? Become more aware of how you use your time and resources.

For example, when Yolanda did these exercises, she noted several possible soft addictions: shopping, surfing chat rooms, nail biting, collecting, and crankiness. After considering each addiction, Yolanda decided that chat rooms, shopping, nail biting, and crankiness were probably soft addictions for her, but collecting was not. Collecting Native American beadwork and artifacts sometimes gave her a "rush," but she primarily used it to deepen her understanding and appreciation of her heritage. Realizing her motivations, feelings, and the time she spent on these activities was very enlightening. She noticed her collecting felt inspiring and grounded as opposed to her nervous nail biting, compulsive shopping, and habitual crankiness. She realized how consuming her cyber-conversations had become and how the "buzz" of anonymous conversation was replacing face-to-face encounters.

By now, you probably have a good idea of what your soft addictions are. Your awareness will continue to grow. You might start by saying them out loud: "I am a daydreamer." "I watch way too much television." "I obsess about my hair." "I can't stop complaining about my life."

As difficult as it might be to verbalize your soft addictions, saying them out loud can be cathartic. While saying them doesn't mean you're rid of them, it can give you a sense of relief and release. Talking and sharing are parts of the process of living a highly conscious life. They help turn soft addictions from dirty little secrets into honest acknowledgments of how you've been spending your time and energy. The sharing can feel great.

A WEB RATHER THAN A LIST

As you identify your soft addictions, you'll discover that a mere list doesn't do them justice. Soft addictions aren't linear; they're more like a web of interconnecting strands. As you identify your addictions and do the exercises in this book, you'll start to see how your soft addictions interconnect, and how one leads to another. For instance, you drink a ton of coffee and get jittery. So you bite your nails and nosh on pretzels. You try to calm down, and end up zoning out in front of the television. In other instances, the connection between addictions is subtle. For example, you may identify the following as addictions: dieting, going to clubs nightly, playing games like solitaire, reading escapist novels, feeling self-pity, and avoiding making a serious career choice. In and of themselves, these items do not seem like anything to be alarmed about. It's only when viewed in totality—an interconnected drain on time, energy, and spirit—that their power can be glimpsed.

The analogy to a web is appropriate because, like a web, soft addictions entice and lure the unwary, the various strands are connected, and once you're trapped, it's difficult to extricate yourself. Jane, for instance, engages in many different activities and moods, all of which keep her from experiencing the deep pain that lurks below the surface. Reading third-rate romance novels, dieting, and self-pity may not seem to have much in common, except that they all keep her in a steady state. The romance novels provide a mildly pleasant escape, the dieting fosters the illusion of doing something worthwhile (losing weight seems like a good thing to do), and self-pity is a safe, low-level emotional state, which is better than real pain or no feelings at all. If Jane could pull back and view her behaviors and moods from a holistic perspective, she would discover that she devotes almost every second of every day to keeping away from her authentic self.

> ## More to think about
>
> What are the elements of your soft addiction web?

Think about your soft addictions from this holistic viewpoint. They're not just things you do or moods you have but a web of daily routines that hold you back from experiencing the More.

In the next chapter, you'll discover how your mind creates this web of soft addictions.

5.

MINDING YOUR MIND

"Change your thoughts, and you
change your world."
—NORMAN VINCENT PEALE

Minding your mind harnesses the power of your errant thoughts to lead you to a life of More. Like monitoring a playground full of lively children, minding your mind means that you keep tabs on your thoughts as they skip, leap, ramble, and twirl, always keeping an eye out for problems and staying aware of when you need to set limits. A well-monitored mind provides a playground for More.

Clarity of thinking is crucial if we want a life of More. If we are better able to understand our mind and its penchant for unruly thinking—if we're able to spot what we call "stinking thinking" and denial—we can better discern which thoughts lead us to More and avoid those that lead us to less.

The point isn't just to stop a soft addiction but to manage the thinking that leads to and perpetuates it. Without understanding our thinking, we are likely to just replace one soft addiction with another. Minding our mind may be difficult, but it's also a liberating, exhilarating, learning experience. Clarity and truth are the greatest rewards for overcoming soft addictions.

We all use excuses, rationalizations, denial, defensiveness, cons, and cover-ups to perpetuate our less-than-desirable behaviors. These are evidence of our stinking thinking. The degree to which we learn to mind our mind and rein in our stinking thinking and denial is the degree to which we can lead a life of More.

WHY MIND OUR MIND?

Our mind uses our thoughts and beliefs to maintain the status quo. That is because a basic function of our unconscious mind is to preserve our organism by maintaining homeostasis. Soft addictions can be seen as mechanisms of the status quo. They are proven, familiar, safe. When risk and unpredictability threaten our mind, the mind responds with attempts to thwart change and uses our soft addiction routines to dull and protect us. Yet, to live the More, we must learn and grow, taking risks that challenge our security.

Let's see how Sam's thinking was keeping him locked in soft addictions and away from a life of More.

Sam was a night owl. He hated going to bed and would either watch television until he fell asleep or log on to the Internet and shop for books, CDs, DVDs, meet his "cyberfriends," peruse travel sites to "plan" his next vacation or check his investments. Sometimes he would surf the Net and then watch television to put himself to sleep. But he didn't easily sleep. Hooked on late-night programming and channel surfing (hoping to catch a glimpse of flesh on the screen), he often didn't get to sleep until the wee hours of the morning. He then had a tough time getting up in the morning, thinking that it must be his rough days at the office that were creating this problem. He felt like his job held him hostage; after all, who can try to sell day after day and not be burned out? His customers were all demanding, yet they never seemed to be able to make a decision. How could he sign any deals if they didn't know what they wanted? All of these stinking thoughts went through Sam's head on a daily basis.

His sales were lackluster, his performance reviews were mediocre, and his love life was stagnant. His manager suggested that he come to the Institute for sales training.

When he met with the other participants in the sales course, he was surprised to see how many sales they generated, the rate at which they made new contacts, and how they were constantly improving their income. He asked Rob, one of the top producers in the course, how he made so many calls and appointments in one week. Rob told him he took the early morning train into the city and got a jump on his day, planning his calls. As a result, his business hours were a lot more productive and he enjoyed his days more. He said he loved talking to people and making friends every day. He even met his wife that way. Sam said, "I can't get up that early, I'd be too tired. I don't get to bed until 2:00 A.M., so I can't get up at 6:00 A.M. to get ready for work."

When Rob challenged him about his evening routines, Sam insisted, "I need to watch television at night. It's important to watch the news. I have to know what's going on in the world. Then, I need to watch more TV to wind down after a hard day at work and get my mind off my annoying customers. Late-night TV is relaxing for me.

"And, hey, surfing the Net is great! I find great deals, plan exotic vacations, and meet some interesting people at night on the Internet. I've made some really good contacts, and they count on hearing from me each night."

As they talked more, Rob confided his feeling that he was serving his clients, not just closing deals, and that he ends up feeling nourished by them. He said that connecting fully with people left him feeling more engaged and satisfied in his work and home life.

After being around others who were living More and having more fun in their work with great results, Sam stopped rationalizing his soft addictions and began to clean up his stinking thinking. Rather than justifying his routines and hiding from his problems, he admitted he was conning himself.

He started to limit his Internet surfing and television viewing and even moved his television out of his bedroom. He started reading at night, talking with friends, and meditating. He was able to get up earlier in the mornings and get to work before others got there. He felt the extra hour or two in the morning was like getting an extra day. His sales manager was thrilled with his sales performance, and Sam felt more satisfied, too. Once he was able to catch himself in his stinking thinking, Sam shifted his behaviors to create his own life of More.

STINKING THINKING AND DENIAL: WHAT THEY DO

Like Sam, we all use stinking thinking and denial to justify our behavior, avoid feelings, and con others as well as ourselves. Denial, defensiveness, overgeneralization, minimizing, blaming, and jumping to conclusions are just some examples of the stinking thinking to which we are vulnerable. When we don't think clearly and cleanly, we are likely to minimize or even deny that our soft addictions pose problems. Stinking thinking prevents us from viewing our routines objectively and honestly.

Stinking thinking is so pervasive we often don't realize it exists. We think our stinking thoughts are facts, not arbitrary decisions based on faulty beliefs. Our distorted thoughts normalize our soft addiction routines. Stinking thinking becomes like a sea we live in. We're like fish, not knowing water exists around them until they're caught. Stinking thoughts lead us to indulge in soft addictions, defend the behavior, and deny any problem with our actions. Stinking thinking becomes a sort of soft addiction in itself—a habitual thought pattern that we return to repeatedly for diminishing returns.

Soft addictions function as a filter of our experience, screening out useful input. As we enmesh ourselves in shopping, gossiping, and daydreaming routines, we fail to feel the pain that could guide us toward right action. Without feeling our pain, we more easily deny that anything is wrong. The vicious cycle, of course, is that we engage in soft addictions precisely because we don't want to feel pain. Without the ability to see our lives clearly and feel the pain completely, we can convince ourselves that our soft addictions are harmless or even that they are good for us.

That's why we deny with comments like, "What problem? What pain? What do you mean this is a problem? I can't see it as a problem."

We might intellectually know that spending hours on the Internet or buying and reading every gossip magazine are problems. We might know that there is a better way to nourish ourselves than to mindlessly munch M&M's and eat from take-out containers. Yet without our pain available to us, we don't grasp that something profound is happening beneath the surface. We eat, shop, or watch TV in place of taking effective action. We can't feel our spiritual hunger or our yearning to be loved, to matter, and to make a difference.

Fortunately, we can learn to catch ourselves when we overgeneralize or use bizarre logic. If we notice stinking thoughts, we won't fall into the denial trap. When we become aware of our faulty thought processes, we can change our thoughts; when we change our thoughts, we can shift our feelings and behaviors in a more productive, meaningful direction.

HOLD YOUR NOSE: STINKING THINKING

What does stinking thinking sound like, especially as it relates to our soft addiction routines? Let's look at some of Sam's stinking thinking:

More to do

Rent *Monty Python and the Holy Grail* and watch the infamous bridge scene. In true Python fashion, the lone guard depicts denial clearly. Significantly outnumbered, he asserts he can win the battle even as he loses limb after limb, claiming they are "merely flesh wounds" and cause him no pain.

"I don't have a problem."

"I can't get up early."

"My customers are never satisfied."

"Joe stays up later than I do, and he doesn't find nearly as many bargains on eBay."

"I only surfed the Web for half an hour last night."

"I'll work on getting to bed earlier after I close this big account."

"That customer is not going to pay on time—I just know it."

"It's not my fault the sale fell through."

"I can't fall asleep without visiting the chat room to see what is happening tonight."

"I need to watch all the news every day."

When we become defensive or use the above rationalizations for any of these purposes, chances are we are in the grip of a soft addiction. If we weren't in a mood, thought, or behavioral addiction, we wouldn't defend or rationalize so stubbornly. We would talk freely about the behavior or mood, ask questions about its source, and consider changing the way we're thinking or acting. Ultimately, we might decide not to change but we would be truthful about the addiction.

> ## More to do
>
> Which of Sam's thoughts are like yours? How often do you or your friends express these or similar types of thoughts?

Consider the following two responses when someone is confronted about how much time they spend reading the newspaper each day:

A. "Yeah, I see that my reading the newspaper cover to cover every day is taking a lot of time—plus the time I spend doing the crossword puzzle. I probably could use the time better."

B. "I need to read the newspaper every day. I have to keep up. It is important to be an educated citizen. I might miss something otherwise. I think it's weird that other people can get through the day without knowing about what's going on around them; I don't know how you can stand to be uninformed. In fact, if there were more people like you, it would be easy for dictators to gain power because there's nothing they like better than an uninformed populace."

The second quote has a defensive tone and communicates, "Back off, I don't want to discuss this." The speaker goes on the offensive to throw off the questioner. He also denies any possible cost of his behavior and sees no other possibility. While being an educated citizen is certainly important, this person uses the argument as a defense rather than a truly thoughtful examination of the best ways to be informed.

When you're locked into soft addiction routines, these excuses, justifications, defensive remarks, and rationalizations become verbal reflexes. When threatened with exposure of your soft addiction, you respond with some form of denial. In many instances, your response is so convincing that it's difficult for anyone to refute. It serves its intended purpose of backing people off, stopping any exploration, and preventing you from examining something you're attached to in a limiting way.

Recognizing our stinking thinking unblocks us and moves us in the right direction. When we identify these counterproductive patterns, we're in a better position to change them so they're in alignment with our One Decision. We open our eyes to all aspects of More—all the life, love, and meaning—that exist in the world.

STINKING THINKING: A FILTER

Why would anyone think the way Sam does? Because deep down inside, what we believe about ourselves is, "I am not okay," "It's not okay to feel my feelings," "I'm different," "I can't have what I want," "I don't have what it takes to get through a rough situation."

Acknowledging our soft addictions means confronting these fears and doubts. If we really want more, we need to invite others to give us truthful feedback, catch ourselves in convoluted thinking, and identify the negative impact it has on our lives. Instead, we rationalize, deny, and defend our soft addictions.

As a result, stinking thinking prevents us from mindfully assessing our behavior in light of our higher values and goals. In fact, we don't question our behavior, ignoring the niggling challenges at the edges of our consciousness that question how we're acting. Since our feelings and consciousness are muted, we don't realize that we are doing things that are not productive or things that are even harmful.

Kelly is an attractive woman inside and out. She has what her friends call "a good heart," and she is a straight shooter in business. Kelly, however, was caught in her own web of stinking thinking and soft addictions.

Kelly was passed over for a promotion at a marketing agency. She originally accepted her job with this company because of its reputation for good business and the value it placed on developing its employees. She was particularly impressed by her boss's reputation as a fair businessman. When Kelly's boss informed her that her coworker had received the promotion, he also told Kelly how much he believed in and appreciated her. He pointed out that Kelly was also on track for promotion because of her integrity and ability to get the best out of her employees. He explained that he wanted to help develop Kelly for another job that was better suited to her career path.

> ## More alert
>
> Stinking thinking can be costly. Perhaps you've talked yourself out of asking for a promotion, postponed career moves, assumed people would reject you and didn't make the sales you could, or blamed others for your situation rather than doing what you could to generate and receive more abundance. . . . Notice how stinking thinking creates less, not More.

Kelly, though, only saw that she didn't get this immediate promotion. She thought, *I'll never get that promotion in the future. My boss was just dangling me along. I knew it wouldn't work. He doesn't value my work. I should never have taken this job.* As a result of this thinking, Kelly started to show up late for work, take long lunches, and spend long periods zoning out, poring over fashion magazines, and reading newspapers from cover to cover. She shifted her life away from a path toward More and headed into her soft addiction routines.

Rather than face her hurt, insecurity, and disappointment or discuss the situation with her boss, Kelly indulged her mood addictions of hopelessness and self-pity, her avoidance addictions of procrastination and being late, and her activity addictions of reading fashion magazines and newspapers. You can begin to see that her thinking stinks and is not based on the truth but on her faulty perceptions.

If Kelly had been aware of the different types of stinking thinking that trip people up, she would have been in a better position to identify them and limit their negative impact. These ways of stinking thinking not only keep us locked into soft addiction routines but also actually make us susceptible to soft addictions in the first place.

MIND MANEUVERS

As we learn to recognize the many forms stinking thinking takes, we understand how it justifies and perpetuates soft addictions. Identifying our thought patterns helps us analyze and counter them. Because so many people deny their stinking thinking, it's only fitting that we start with denial.

The Many Faces of Denial

Refusal to admit that something exists or that it has a negative impact is denial. For instance we don't recognize our soft addiction or stinking thinking as a problem. To keep our denial intact, we resort to defensiveness, rationalizing, lying, minimizing, postponing, and comparing to explain, justify, or put off what we deny.

Defensiveness crops up when someone mentions our soft addiction routines and we reflexively defend whatever activities or moods have us entangled. Even if someone isn't accusatory but simply questions if we do too much of this or that—we respond as if we were indicted.

"Don't even suggest that my Tom Cruise fantasies aren't good for me. They're what I look forward to and I don't think it's fair that you're questioning me about them."

Rationalization involves creating superficially convincing and often ingenious arguments about why soft addiction routines aren't bad, and even why they are good. It explains and justifies.

"Maybe I do shop a lot, but I've got to have the right look to get ahead in the business world."

More to do

Rent the movie *The Devil's Advocate* to see the slippery slope of soft addictions and denial in action. (Al Pacino plays the devil and seduces Keanu Reeves's character using soft addictions as a lure.) Use it to recognize your stinking thinking and break your own denial by identifying similarities with all of the characters. See it with friends and discuss it afterward.

Minimizing is when we act like a soft addiction really isn't a problem, or if it is, it's not a big one.

Trivializing the activity or downplaying a common mood is a sure sign of minimizing.

"It's only a little bit of gossip. It's not as if that's all I do."

Lying is an extreme form of minimizing. Fibbing about the scope and depth of our soft addiction routines keeps our denial going. While we lie to ourselves, we usually lie to others. We insist that we only shop one day a week when we know perfectly well that we go to the mall at least three times weekly, or we tell a friend or spouse that we don't enjoy wallowing in self-pity when in fact we take a perverse comfort in these "woe is me" moments.

"I don't watch a lot of television."

"I haven't done that since we talked last month."

"No, that couldn't have been me that you saw at the mall."

"I didn't take the last piece of cake."

Postponing generally goes hand in hand with minimizing. It involves admitting our soft addictions aren't good for us, but putting off resolving the problem. We excuse current soft addictions by making a vague promise to do something about them in the future.

"I know I'm wasting a lot of time reading catalogues, but when I quit my job next year, I'm going to change what I do in my spare time."

Comparing is a particularly subtle form of denial. To put ourselves in a better light, we excuse our routines by comparing them more favorably to others who have even worse soft addictions.

"I may go to the health club a little too much, but that's nothing compared to that guy who is there every single day from open to close."

SNIFFING OUT OTHER STINKING THINKING

Denial and its many forms are the most formidable stinking thinking gambits. Denial keeps us from putting our One Decision into action. It must be overcome if we are to truly live the More.

More subtle—and sometimes more difficult to detect and neutralize—are the other forms of stinking thinking. They often seem so reasonable and their seduction so appealing that we can counter them only with extreme clarity and vigilance. Learn and beware.

Overgeneralizing

We often miss possibilities because we view a negative event as a never-ending pattern. Instead of seeing a negative situation as a unique event, we view it through a trick mirror that produces infinite images. We magnify and blow things out of proportion, imagine things are impossible, have hopeless thoughts, and think in extremes often characterized by all or nothing terms like "always" and "never."

"This *always* happens."

"I blew it. I ate a hot fudge sundae, so my diet is ruined. I might as well _____."

"I won't be able to limit my television watching no matter what I do."

"I'll never lose weight."

Jumping to Conclusions or Irrational Conclusions

Deciding that things are bad without sufficient evidence leads us to jump to conclusions. Instead of focusing on desired outcomes and how to achieve them, we will even use a mental filter, ignoring positive or contradictory information in order to stick to our negative predictions. We mind-read and assume negative reactions or fortune-tell negative outcomes. We project things we are feeling onto others. We also use magical thinking, imagining connections where none exist.

"They are going to fire me."

"She doesn't like me, so why bother to look nice."

"This isn't going to work out, so I should just quit and go to the video arcade."

"I'll never get that raise."

"You don't like me." (In reality, I don't like you, but I am addicted to playing nice with you.)

"I did a horrible job. I answered that last question totally wrong. I flunked the test."

"I'll retire by winning the lottery."

Emotional Reasoning

This form of stinking thinking involves reasoning based on how you feel without comparing it to reality. It occurs when people think that because they feel a certain way, that is the way it is. Then they overgeneralize or jump to conclusions.

"I feel stupid therefore I must be stupid."

"This chapter feels fragmented: it will never come together."

"I feel upset, so I must be a mess."

"I don't feel good, so there must be something wrong with me."

Should and Shouldn't Statements

When we criticize ourselves or others with should, shouldn't, must, ought, and have to, we moralize the behavior. Shoulds and shouldn'ts reduce behavior to simplistic values like good or bad. This form of thinking often leads us to affix blame or avoid responsibility.

"He should have fixed that."

"I ought to have that handled by now."

"I have to have that."

Blame/Shame

Blaming is often linked to overgeneralizing and should/shouldn't. You blame yourself for something you weren't entirely responsible for or you blame others and disregard what you contributed. You overlook accurate attribution of responsibility and actually keep correction from happening with thoughts like:

"It's all my fault."

"You ruined it!"

"I didn't do it."

Labeling

This form of stinking thinking occurs when you name-call or when you attribute limited qualities to yourself and others. When relating to yourself, instead of saying, "I made a mistake," you tell yourself, "I am a loser," "I am stupid," "I am a jerk." When categorizing or name-calling others, we think things like: "He's a fool." "What do you expect from a capitalist?" This keeps you from learning and taking effective, corrective action.

The mind is infinitely creative in developing categories of stinking thinking. Stay alert and see how many others you can find. A few others that I find amusing include:

Irrelevant excuses: "I hadn't had my coffee when that happened."

Silly rules: "I already went to the bank. I can't retrace my steps today."

Funny logic: "If I eat peanut butter and jelly on toast, it is not the same as having a peanut butter and jelly sandwich, so it doesn't count as much."

More to think about

What "stinking thoughts" have you had while reading this section?

Limited thinking: "I can't do it." "It's never been done before." "I'm not capable."

Scarcity thinking: "It's because I don't have enough time, money, or resources to change." "If I only had more help, I could do this."

CLEANING UP YOUR STINKING THINKING

Becoming aware of your thinking is essential to creating More. If you are aware of the stinking thinking you are winning already.

To increase your ability to recognize stinking thinking, you might want to:

Watch a movie and pick out stinking thinking. Make a scorecard with the major categories and put a hatch mark on it for every one you catch.

Use the same scorecard for yourself. Set up a tape recorder in your house near your phone. Switch it on the next time a friend calls and record your part of the conversation. Listen to your conversation and keep score of your own stinking thinking. In what ways do you limit yourself?

Watch for stinking thinking in everyday conversation—yours and others. Better yet, if you are feeling adventuresome, point it out and discuss it with friends. Be prepared to deal with their initial defensiveness.

LIGHTEN UP TO THINK MORE CLEARLY

You don't need to get rid of your stinking thinking; you need to moderate it with humor and compassion.

With a sense of humor and compassion for our personal flaws, we find it easier to see and accept how our behavior is misaligned with our dreams. Humor gives us the distance and space necessary to admit that there's something wrong with our soft addiction routines.

None of us likes to feel stupid or looks forward to admitting a mistake. It's doubly difficult to admit these feelings or mistakes when we can't laugh at or forgive ourselves. Main-

taining a sense of humor promotes the compassion that facilitates questioning, examining, growing, and changing our behavior. With compassion and humor, we admit less than desirable things about ourselves and still know that we are okay human beings. We don't have to lie or deny to protect ourselves. We can face the unattractive parts of ourselves— our flaws and unflattering needs—with greater equanimity.

Bart, for instance, used to be embarrassed about his soft addiction routines. Every night he vegged out, just sitting in a kind of stupor on the couch looking at nothing in particular. It was a perverse kind of meditation, one in which he simply disappeared instead of going inward. When not vegging out, he spent a lot of time ogling women and fantasizing about them. For a while, Bart reacted negatively when his roommate mentioned these routines and suggested he might find

a better use for his time. He covered his embarrassment by insisting he needed to be a couch potato after a hard day at work and that his fantasies harmed no one.

Only when he came to the Institute did he move away from reflexive denial and stinking thinking. We encouraged him to accept, forgive, and laugh at himself more. He regularly forgave himself for a behavior or a thought. After a month or two, Bart stopped automatically denying that his addiction routines were unnecessary and harmful. Though he didn't immediately stop vegging out and fantasizing about women, he gradually acknowledged that he wasted precious time and energy on these activities. He found himself more willing to talk with his fiancée about his insecurities and about the love and reassurance he wanted from a relationship.

Bart made a conscious effort to find something funny about his life on a daily basis; he'd write a sentence describing the humor in one of his actions or thoughts. He told us about his special babe-watching rating scale from zero to five, with zero as "look away fast" and five being a panting drool akin to Pavlov's dog. He regaled us with stories about the number of five-glance women in summer that sent him to the chiropractor for neck adjustments because of abrupt rubber-necked glances. We began to look forward to hearing these absurdities from him. Making fun of himself gave him the distance to look at himself objectively and begin dealing with his soft addictions. He even took improvisation classes and had some success at stand-up comedy. Though Bart still falls back on his soft addictions at times, he sees them for what they are and jokes about them. With humor and compassion, Bart moved himself away from his addiction routines and toward More.

DEVELOPING YOUR SENSE OF HUMOR

Transitioning to a life of More is a huge challenge for any of us. It can be especially challenging for those with perfectionist personalities. Without humor, living your One Decision can feel like an impossible challenge rather than an invitation to More. Most of us, though, will benefit if we make a conscious effort to ease up on ourselves and laugh at the things we do. Here are a few techniques for developing self-acceptance, compassion, and a sense of humor.

Keep a humor journal. Use your imagination to creatively and lightly examine yourself. Write something funny you said or did. Use it to gain distance on something you felt bad about. Make fun of your neurotic tendencies or your workaholism. Create a satirical sketch about how you acted. Draw a picture that pokes fun at yourself. While your entries might seem forced at first, you'll gradually have fun with it. And it will help you to stop taking everything you do so seriously.

Creatively express your humor. Put different words to a popular song, with lyrics reflecting your soft addiction routines. Draw a cartoon about yourself. Create a pseudonym for yourself and write an anecdote that captures you at your most absurd. Write a ridiculous news story about your soft addiction routine: "Josie won the snooze alarm Olympics today. She faced tough competition, but after twenty-nine hits delivered with perfect style, she was declared the winner. She received double technical credit for the slap and punch technique that sent the alarm flying across the room."

Practice daily forgiveness. At the end of each day, grant yourself a pardon for whatever "sin" you think you committed. Review what you beat yourself up for—missing a workout or a deadline, having an argument with a friend, spending too much or too little, losing your keys, etc.—and choose one thing for which you feel you deserve forgiveness. Then say out loud an affirmation that communicates your forgiveness: "I forgive myself for spending so much time searching the Web for a deal on running shoes."

More-sel

Be inspired by someone who has a sense of humor about herself: "When choosing between two evils, I always like to take the one I've never tried before."

—MAE WEST

More to do

Read *Confessions of a Shopaholic* by Sophie Kinsella or *Rachel's Holiday* by Marian Keyes for a humorous view of stinking thinking. See if you can relate to the main characters' hilarious rationalizations and loopy thinking.

THE STINKING THINKING TEMPLATE

Any time you are having stinking thoughts, you can use the following template to "reprogram" your thinking. Students at the Institute often use this to clean up their thoughts. You can find an interactive version of this template on our Web site, *www.theremustbemore.com*.

1. What event or situation triggered your stinking thinking? What soft addiction(s) did you turn to?

2. What feelings were you having?

3. What thoughts were going through your head during or after this event? How do those thoughts keep you from pursuing More?

4. What positive thoughts could you think instead (thoughts reflecting the reality of the situation, or thoughts that are humorous, compassionate, or forgiving)?

As you look over your responses, can you see your soft addictions with greater clarity? Can you see how stinking thinking prevents you from recognizing the routines that cause you to get less out of life?

Stinking thinking stems from our need to explain to ourselves and to others why we live with less, fulfilling our surface wants and never really feeling satisfied. These thoughts keep us from really knowing ourselves. Being aware of your stinking thinking can lead you to discover the mistaken beliefs you have about yourself and the world, leading to much self-knowledge and understanding. In the next chapter, you'll learn to appreciate your more essential self by unearthing the deep-rooted reason for your soft addictions: the Why.

6.

THE WHY: CRACKING YOUR OWN CODE

"The basic principle of spiritual life is
that our problems become the very place to
discover wisdom and love."
—JACK KORNFIELD

Beneath each soft addiction routine, a treasure awaits our discovery. Decoded, every aspect of our soft addictions— our activities, the substances we use, and our feelings right before we indulge—reveals key information. All soft addictions have a positive intent because they spring from a desire to take care of ourselves. Ironically, though, these addictive routines prevent us from actually taking good care of ourselves by masking the underlying problems. They prevent us from reading the information that our system tries to send.

The Why of our addictions often lies just beyond our conscious reach. We may recognize the urge to indulge a soft addiction, accepting superficial analyses (*I'm bored. I need a break*) as if they really explain our behavior. We respond to our stinking thinking and miss the deeper Why: Why do I want a soft addiction at this moment? Why do I have this soft addiction routine? Why did I develop this pattern? We don't often see the deeper needs—yearning for comfort, hungering to matter, and longing to feel significant—underneath the surface urges. In fact, as we saw in the preceding chapter, our stinking thinking functions to buffer us from those powerful yearnings. Yet, it's when we finally embrace our underlying needs and fears that we are better able to seek the More.

DIRECTING THE FLOW

Prepare to uncover a powerful emotional force when you unearth the Why—the underlying needs—beneath your soft addictions. That's because deep feelings are embedded in those needs.

More alert

You may be taking the damper off emotions as you discover your Why. Go toward your feelings and experience them fully. As powerful as they are, you are stronger. If you run away from your feelings, you'll fail to harness their power and be likely to slip back into your routines. There are no bad feelings, only underdeveloped skills in dealing with them. Get support and build the skills to become More you.

Soft addiction routines are a way we have of regulating our energy or the flow of life through us. Our emotions comprise a big part of our life energy. If we don't like our strong emotions and desires, or think we must contain them, we try to manage that flow through soft addiction routines. Soft addictions function like the resistor in a stereo, which channels and damps down the electrical energy flowing in. It takes in and resists the full 110 volts arriving at the system, letting in only the level of electrical charge that the stereo can work with.

In a similar way, when we don't have the capacity to handle the flow of emotions and desires pouring through our body, we "resist" our life energy by numbing ourselves with a soft addiction routine. The result is a "kinda-checked-out" state of low emotion that we accept as normal. But it's not normal. Look at young children; they aren't checked out. They have lots of emotions, which they express freely. The checked-out state is a behavior we've learned in place of developing the ability to direct our life energy. When we acknowledge the hungers beneath our routines, then we can expand our capacity to let life flow through us.

WHY THE WAITRESS IS STUCK IN HER NUTTY ROUTINE

I am sitting in a restaurant working on this book. I notice that my waitress, Donna, keeps retracing her path in and out of the kitchen, emerging each time with a handful of nuts. Donna has only a few customers in the restaurant, so I start a conversation with her. She mentions that she is eating handfuls of nuts out of boredom. "I'm not even hungry, yet I can't seem to stop, and I keep grabbing them every time."

This instance of Donna's behavior alone doesn't signal a soft addiction; we would need to know more about Donna and her various routines. However, Donna's actions do tell us a lot about why we fall into soft addiction routines. Donna is bored and so she eats too many nuts. She may be feeling anxious about the empty time, the lack of business, and the lack of tip money. She may be upset about any number of things, yet all she registers consciously is that she is "bored," so she keeps returning to the kitchen and the nut bowl.

> ### More to do
>
> Try analyzing the Why behind a friend or loved one's soft addictions. Write down this person's addiction routines and speculate about the deeper reasons he or she is drawn to these particular routines.

Fritz Perls, the founder of American Gestalt Psychology, saw boredom as withheld anger.[3] I believe it can result from other repressed emotions, too. Donna told me that she loved her job but found it difficult to focus when it was slow.

3. Frederick S. Perls, *The Gestalt Approach and Eyewitness to Therapy* (Palo Alto, Calif.: Science & Behavior Books, 1973).

She said, "It's hard to feel like I have meaning on a day like today. I'm just filling time." Clearly, Donna was afraid of feeling worthless and perhaps poor. She attempted to numb her fear with boredom and by raiding the nut bowl.

Donna's Why isn't boredom—that's just a surface explanation. By going deeper into Donna's nut routine, we find that she's hungry for security, to make a difference, to feel useful and engaged. She could create more ways of meeting her real, deeper hunger if she could see what she really hungers for. She would then establish more fulfilling contact with customers, make better friends with the staff, or even ask for more responsibility. As a result of her increased involvement, she might receive a promotion, become a manager, and learn to deal with her own employees' boredom.

THE ORIGIN OF SOFT ADDICTION ROUTINES: MISTAKEN BELIEFS

Donna's raiding of the nut bowl has a point of origin in her past. In fact, most of our soft addiction routines can be traced back to two aspects of our youth. These are the behaviors or attitudes we learned for dealing with the world, plus our mistaken beliefs about ourselves and the world around us.

As children we learn to do things like hold back our tears, deny fear, repress anger, and even restrain joy and love in the face of family disapproval or discomfort. To deal with the feelings we learned to hold back, we might reach for a candy bar or a book, go off and hide, or collapse in self-pity— the beginnings of our soft addiction routines. Back then, our routines protected us or brought us much needed comfort. We did not believe there were alternative ways to act.

From our childhood experiences we formed beliefs about ourselves and the world. We decided whether we were lovable or unlovable; if the world was safe or dangerous; and if others were interested in our satisfaction or not. We often formed mistaken beliefs from our limited viewpoint. From these mistaken beliefs our stinking thinking grows, and in turn spawns our soft addictions.

As young children with few available resources, our soft addiction routines were creative adaptations to a tough situation. As adults, we have other resources for coping with comparable difficulties. Yet we tend to fall back upon those deeply ingrained habits from childhood and blow right past other choices. It's as if, in some ways, we still see the world through the eyes of a child. We try our softly addictive behaviors again and again, unconsciously thinking they will eventually work. We create an addictive routine by applying ineffective solutions to undefined, unrecognized problems.

Had we all grown up in situations that fostered direct expression of our feelings and provided comfort and encouragement, we would express ourselves more directly and effectively today. We would have learned to talk through our feelings and concerns and receive appropriate guidance, feedback, or comfort instead of turning to soft addiction routines. As adults, we have the power we lacked as children to understand our deeper hurts and longings and address them directly. But we're also fighting deeply ingrained behaviors. And, in many ways, our society promotes soft addictions by discouraging dealing effectively with our emotions. We are rewarded, indirectly, for hanging on to our stinking thinking.

Let me share stories with you from my life and others' to help you discover the breeding ground for your soft addictions. You can see how childhood experiences evolve into adult soft addictions. The stories also explain how it's possible to extricate ourselves from our routines by linking early experiences with specific soft addictions.

> ## More-sel
>
> "Your past forms you, whether you like it or not. Each encounter and experience has its own effect, and you're shaped the way the wind shapes a mesquite tree on a plain."
> —LANCE ARMSTRONG

As I looked more closely at my own soft addiction routines of zoning out with reading, television, and snacks, I discovered myself as a chubby little girl. I saw myself idly watching television after school, eating bags of chocolate chip cookies, drinking cartons of milk, and scribbling homework. When I looked even closer, I saw a lonely girl with upsets she couldn't share or express. I could sense distress and tension within and around me as if there were an undertow lurking below the seemingly calm surface. I didn't want to add to the tensions or upset in the house, yet there were feelings and situations I couldn't "stomach." I began to eat to fill my tummy so that I didn't feel the churnings inside. I effectively numbed myself from the upset. In my loneliness, I hungered for connection and more relationship with people. I didn't find it in the world around me, so I sought it in the world of books and television. These patterns continued into my adulthood. I now know, when I have an urge to indulge in a soft addiction, to look inside for the little girl who is hungering for reassurance and comfort. I know she deserves attention and company, the kind that God and I can give her.

Bob

I saw another great example in my husband's life. When we got married, Bob told me he didn't have a television because he was addicted to it. I didn't believe that until I observed Bob watching TV, completely lost to himself as he flipped constantly between two and three programs, shutting me out even as I struggled to make conversation with him in thirty-second bites during commercials. (We no longer have a television in our house, other than a little twelve-inch TV/VCR we keep in a closet.) When Bob asked his mother about the origins of his television addiction, she responded, "When you were little, your father couldn't tolerate the messes that little kids make. We got our first TV when you were four and your sister was one and a half. I noticed that when we snacked in front of the television, your father didn't fuss over you kids. So, I began serving dinner on TV trays. Your father's silence was a relief." Bob's mother didn't realize that soft addictions begin as a misguided attempt to deal with unwanted emotions. Rather than letting meals be a time for the family to talk or for children to receive attention, at Bob's childhood home they became a time to manage their father's upset and anxiety by putting everything into a haze. Bob learned to eat away anxiety. Wanting to zone out at mealtime is still a much greater issue for him than for me. He has learned to manage it, but the urge to merge with the television still pulses strongly within him.

Heather

Heather's soft addiction routines revolve around shopping, looking good, and overspending on designer clothing. As she looked more deeply at her urges to shop, she realized that, as a child, she had received a lot of positive attention for being pretty. Whenever she felt insecure or unloved, she would dress up to get attention. Her mother had laid out her clothes for her at night until she was twelve years old. Heather concluded that it didn't matter how well she did things; what mattered was how she looked. Since Heather couldn't satisfy her hunger to be understood and valued by her mother, she accepted the substitute of becoming her mother's little doll. Today she still tends to overshop and place too much importance on how she looks, but seeing the Why under her soft addictions now helps her to ask directly for attention and seek contact in positive ways, like calling a friend or asking her husband for a hug. She's even gone back to college as an adult, realizing that she values her mind, not just her appearance.

Discovering the deeper needs and lifelong patterns underneath soft addiction routines creates self-acceptance and compassion. When you are closer to understanding the Why, you develop empathy and understanding for yourself. Soft addictions stop looking like some moral flaw or manifestation of a weak will. You reveal them for what they are—misguided yet often creative attempts to meet a very real and legitimate hunger. I am aware of my hunger to express and make contact. Bob can see his deeper hunger to be positively affirmed, to feel safe and secure, and to talk through things. Heather now sees her hunger to be accepted and loved. We have an increased understanding and empathy for ourselves through recognizing the Why, the situations that bred our beliefs and behaviors. Aware of these deeper hungers, we can begin to develop strategies to meet them. With this knowledge we can make different changes—ones in alignment with our One Decision.

CONNECTING PAST WITH PRESENT

The Why stories you have just read offer a glimpse into the links between our experiences as children and our soft addiction routines as adults—but only a glimpse. It would take many pages to do justice to the complex web that links the events of our pasts to the routines of today. My point is that we first form mistaken beliefs about the world as children. For instance, I decided isolation was the only way to protect myself. In response to his father's upset, Bob concluded that expressing himself fully was bad. Heather made up her mind that her real self was unacceptable and only her appearance mattered. Looking back, we can all identify the points at which we mistakenly decided our feelings were bad and unwanted; we can pinpoint incidents that communicated that people didn't want to hear us; we can see how we might have come to the conclusion that the world was an uncaring place.

Once we gain this perspective on our soft addictions, we're better able to challenge our limiting assumptions. We can accept that we're not bad, weak, or stupid for doing what we do. We can see the positive intent behind our be-haviors, the ways in which we created the patterns as a kind of self-care. This perspective helps us develop compassion for ourselves and create comfort, healing, and a fuller life.

Take a moment and consider the Whys in your past. Per-haps you dealt with the tension in your parents' relationship by tuning out fights. It may have been that watching hours of situation comedies on television or voraciously reading sci-ence fiction novels helped you deal with pain, anger, or fear.

Whatever your experiences as a child, your behaviors were an adaptation to your environment. Today, you're still responding reflexively to that childhood environment, even though you're no longer in it. There is nothing wrong with these responses when they're consciously chosen. The prob-lem is when they are unproductive, habitual, and unconscious responses. The key, therefore, is to make the responses con-scious. Even though many of us have multiple soft addictions to different things, it is likely that a coherent, underlying pattern drives them. As we begin to discover those patterns, we can unlock the errors of our thinking.

THE WHY OF YOUR MOODS

So far, we have mostly discussed soft addiction routines re-lated to activities and things. But soft addictions also take the form of habitual moods and ways of thinking. Just as Donna, the waitress, persisted in a physical activity (visiting the nut bowl) to avoid her true feelings, we develop persis-tent mental habits to escape our emotions and avoid re-sponsibility for our lives.

Maybe the following list can help you identify some of your mood addictions. Do you see yourself in any of these ways of being? (Think about patterns from your childhood and family, too.)

Avoiding or Minimizing: You put your head in the sand, iso-late, or pretend things aren't as important as they really are.

Attacking and Feeling Superior: You criticize, point out others' inadequacies, or put others on the spot.

Self-Pity/Shame/Inferiority: You act like a sad sack, beat yourself up, put yourself down, sink into hopelessness and despair, indulge in self-pity, whine, or feel like a hapless victim.

Passive-Aggressive: You procrastinate, say "yes" without meaning it, or punish people indirectly by withdrawing from them.

Manipulation: By making indirect requests, you shift the focus but never ask directly and forthrightly for what you need and want.

Defensiveness/Lying: You rationalize, justify, distort the truth, deflect, lie by omission, or lie outright.

Obfuscation: You're vague, act spacey, divert attention from yourself, bring in irrelevant information, or make mountains out of molehills.

None of us wants to see ourselves as manipulative or false or hostile. But remember, our mood addictions have the same positive intentions as our addictions to things; namely, we developed them as coping mechanisms in response to our environment.

To help you find the Why behind your addictions to certain ways of being, read what Cindy and John had to say about their discoveries.

Cindy

"A lot of my addictions revolve around negative attention, whether it's lying, being messy, avoiding, procrastinating, or being passive-aggressive. When I look at my childhood, I realize that when I was about six or eight years old, I would get a kind of mindless attention. It was kind of like positive attention, but it was insincere. My parents would toss off a statement like 'Nice job' and then would move on. They engaged more when they gave me negative attention. I learned to have people connect with me by calling me out, criticizing me, and noticing my bad behavior. I hungered for connection and expressed that by being messy, passive-aggressive, and procrastinating, all of which became a pattern."

John

"An addiction of mine that I uncovered is complaining to my wife. I realized that I gripe to her when I want to get her attention. I believe I know in some way that she'll work harder to please me and pay more attention to me if I am unhappy. She expects less, too. That's the payoff, as it was with my mom when I was growing up. I got the most attention from my mom when I was unhappy. No one in my family joked or talked pleasantly. We all complained and only listened to each other's complaints. What a rotten way to get attention when you think of it. It sure held us back."

FOLLOWING THE TRAIL OF SOFT ADDICTIONS: THE FUNCTIONAL WHY

As we've seen, you can find lots of clues to your soft addictions by looking at your past. There's also another way to help spot your unmet needs and adaptive responses. It is to notice what you are feeling in the moment, right before you start heading into one of your soft addiction routines. By observing yourself in the here and now, you'll find triggers—situations, unmet needs, and other factors—that spark certain patterns. Something happens, and you feel a sudden desire to watch television, surf the Internet, daydream, or eat. By following that behavioral trail back to its starting point, like a path of bread crumbs (unless you are a carbohydrate addict!), you can start to spot the Why under your soft addiction routines. You can answer the question, Why am I reaching for my soft addiction in this moment?

One of the people we've worked with at the Wright Institute, Rosa, has done a good job of following this trail.

For a number of years, part of Rosa's routine involved being highly judgmental and arrogant. She lives in a high-rise apartment with a long elevator ride to the lobby. In the past, Rosa would get into the elevator and make snap judgments about everyone riding with her. In her head, she gossiped about them: *Wonder where she slept last night? Look at her ratty coat. Get a haircut, will ya?*

Rosa avoided talking to the people in the elevator. She was too engaged in self-talk. Besides, who would want to get to know the bunch of losers she made them out to be? At the same time, Rosa didn't feel good about herself when she had these thoughts. While she got a little cold comfort from her superiority, her judgments made her feel even more cranky and alone.

After becoming aware of her pattern of attacking and superiority (and learning the skills of More suggested in this book), Rosa cracked her addiction code. She recognized that her judgmental thoughts were red flags—signals of underlying upset and fear. Rosa put others down to give her ego a boost and mask her sense of inferiority.

Now when she recognizes that she is starting to indulge in gossipy thoughts and negative judgments, Rosa understands that she's really feeling insecure about herself and scared about her day. She has learned a better alternative: she can face her fear and soothe herself. She reassures herself that she is strong enough to handle the day, plan for obstacles and problems that come her way, and reach out for support if she needs it.

Rosa turned awareness of her mental patterns (judging others) into a cue to look at her feelings and name her "demons" of the moment. Luckily, she has a long elevator ride! This self-awareness helps her unlock her mood, and she becomes more engaged in the present. As Rosa treats herself more kindly, she finds she also has more compassion for others. Now, instead of mentally criticizing everyone, she finds herself wishing them a good day or saying a silent prayer for them. Rosa is starting to feel nourished by being part of the human race, not separate from or above it.

CRACKING YOUR CODE

Like Rosa, you're ready to begin cracking your soft addiction routine code. You have the tools to figure out why you do everything from fantasizing to overshopping to slinking into self-pitying moods. By thinking about the issues raised earlier—your childhood experiences, your patterns of behavior—you have already cracked some of the code. Just becoming aware of how your soft addictions correspond to events and actions in your past and your present may have started you thinking in the right direction. You're catching glimpses of the Why.

To formalize this process, the following exercises will help you systematically crack your soft addictions' code.

Write a "Dear John" Letter to Your Addiction

Writing is a great tool to discover facets of yourself and your soft addictions. When our students write letters to specific addictions as if they were people, they often understand why they are drawn to them.

The following exercise is a powerful tool for articulating the bigger Why of your soft addictions. In it, you'll write a letter (or letters, if you choose to write to more than one soft addiction) to your soft addiction. Make sure that you address the following:

1. Tell your soft addiction why you're breaking up with it, as if the addiction were a former boyfriend or girlfriend.

2. Compliment the addiction on its positive intent, how it was trying—but failing—to satisfy a deeper need.

3. Describe the negative effects the addiction has had on your life.

4. Use humor and compassion to explain why you're breaking up.

The following are real letters written by students at the Institute. They may help you craft your own.

Dear Drama Queen,

It is time for us to part ways. I know the main things you have been trying to give me are love and attention and, occasionally, pity. You are so charming. You've been in my family for a long time and I feel so close to you that I am not sure where you begin and I end. We've even had fun together in some pretty convincing performances.

As afraid as I am to admit it, it is time for us to part ways. That doesn't mean that I am not grateful for the purpose you served in the past. As a kid, drama was a way to get attention from a single mom and parent of four. You helped me as a new kid in school, and you even helped me meet people in college. But as an adult, you no longer serve me. You create negative attention and almost trick me into believing the stories you tell: that I deserve pity and that I am not worthy of God's love. You almost had me convinced that this is all that is possible and that I can't have more.

Well, you're wrong. I can have more! I am enough! I am worthy of love and until I start filling it inside me, the hunger will never be met.

So, thank you. Bless you for serving me as a kid, and good-bye.

Pauline

P.S. I am pretty mad at all the time you've wasted in my life. Don't show your ugly face back here again!

Dear Virginia Slims,

Thank you for providing me with years of service as a pacifier and an icebreaker.

Back when I first started dating you, I was just a kid— anxious and dying to be cool. You were my way to calm my fears, give me something to do, make contact (it's easy to ask for a match), and fit in.

Over the years you've continued to comfort me. Now, when I suck in smoke, it's like sucking on a pacifier or my thumb.

I'm finding that I can no longer afford this relationship. Not just that you're no longer a cheap date, but you're really not good for me. I don't breathe as well, I cough more, and my endurance is less. Not only that, I smell bad.

Worry not for me, I'm finding other ways to soothe myself and give myself something to do with my hands. I'm not saying I'm leaving you totally just yet. But it won't be long.

I've loved you a long time and it's time to say good-bye.

> *Love, adieu,*
> *Charity*

P.S. Mr. Coffee, I really can't see you as much, either. I want to say a slow good-bye. You and I have seen a lot of each other. But I want to play with Mr. Tea and Ms. Juice now. Thank you.

Dear Daydreaming,

I've had many good times with you. You helped me escape when I couldn't go anywhere as a kid. I could forget my troubles for a while. I could imagine I was big and strong and could beat up the bullies who chased me.

It can be fun to daydream and think of faraway lands. However, there's a time and a place for everything. Realistically speaking, I overuse you. Instead of using you to run wild with my imagination, I use you to deaden my consciousness. That may be okay when I'm relaxing. But at work, I can't function at my best when I'm not being productive and having fun. In addition, my daydreaming affects other important parts of my life.

I forget to do chores, run errands, talk to people, pay attention to my social life, etc. I pay a very steep price for you and I can't afford to pay the price anymore. I have to go now. Take care.

Thanks,
John

Releasing Ritual

After writing your letters, you may want to conduct the following ritual. Burn the letters and release them to the ether, to spirit, to the wind, to the universe, or whatever you wish. As they burn, affirm that you are releasing your soft addiction. Acknowledge their positive intent and the job they have done. Reassure them that you will take over and find other ways to care for yourself in more fulfilling ways. And let go.

"WHY NOW?" EXERCISES

Writing your "Dear John" letter helps you understand the historical Why of your soft addictions in a compassionate and humorous way. It shows why you have adopted certain patterns in your life and helps you release unproductive patterns.

Here are exercises to help pin down the functional or in-the-moment Why. Use them to track what you are thinking and feeling right as you start to engage in one of your soft addictions. You'll begin to understand why you choose certain soft addictions at particular times. It's like being a detective on your own trail!

The Soft Addiction Path Exercise

Follow the trail to your soft addiction. Imagine that you are on a treasure hunt and knowledge about your soft addiction is the gold. To find this treasure, you'll look for the feelings you were trying to numb or the situation you were trying to avoid as the urge to indulge in one of your soft addictions arose. Unlocking your code really is just a matter of being curious about what's going on inside. The more you do it, the more information you'll receive about your Why.

Scan your day today and pick a soft addiction you indulged in. Then ask yourself:

1. What event, situation, or circumstance triggered my soft addiction? What was I doing or thinking about before I reached for a soft addiction?

2. What was I feeling (any upsetting feelings, uncomfortable emotions)?

3. What mistaken beliefs about the world, myself, and others do I have that may have triggered my stinking thinking and soft addictions?
      Was I acting like I am worthy, beloved, or precious?
      Did I treat my emotions like they were important?
      Did I feel like there was support for me? Do I think that the world is a caring place?

You will begin to see how your soft addiction routines may be tied to certain beliefs, feelings, or even situations. In seeing the connections, you can start to unlock your soft addictions. If you want more practice, visit our Web site, *www.theremustbemore.com*, for a full, interactive template to lead you down the soft addiction path to the path of More.

Create Your Own Soft Addiction Thesaurus

As you do the previous exercise, you're going to find that your various soft addiction moods and behaviors consistently relate to underlying feelings. It's important to become aware of these feelings. To develop this awareness, create a thesaurus. On one side of a sheet of paper, list the soft addiction. On the other side, write the corresponding feeling. For instance:

SOFT ADDICTION BEHAVIOR/ MOOD	FEELING
Elevator judgments	Insecurity/feel bad about self/scared about my day
Gossiping	Loneliness
Working out excessively	Anger/resentment
Fantasizing about movie stars	Feeling unloved
Constant complaining about work	Fear of change

Carry your thesaurus with you as a reference to the underlying feelings when you catch yourself in a soft addiction. Add to it as you continue to follow your soft addiction path. When you find yourself indulging in your soft addictions, pull out your thesaurus. It will remind you of the feelings that lie beneath your soft addictions. Think about what you could do instead to tend to your feelings, comfort yourself, or better prepare for a situation. Remember, you and your emotions are valuable and deserve to be treated with care.

To crack the code of our soft addictions, we've explored the Why—our mistaken beliefs, ingrained habits, mood addictions, personal history, and present-day pressures. We've learned that there are deeper hungers under our soft addictions. We can now learn to identify and fulfill them.

More to think about

Jungians say that alcoholics drink spirits because they crave spirit. Perhaps you gobble up sweets because you crave more sweetness and treats in your life. What other possibilities do you see?

7.

FULFILLING YOUR SPIRITUAL HUNGERS

"It seems to me we can never give up longing
and wishing while we are alive. There are
certain things we feel to be beautiful and good,
and we must hunger for them."
—GEORGE ELIOT

Spiritual hungers are the essential desires that drive our quest for More. They are the deepest and most important needs we have. Paradoxically, they are also the needs we are least trained to meet.

How we relate to these hungers defines our lives. The degree to which we are aware of our hunger determines our degree of satisfaction and fulfillment, our contribution to life, our impact, and our experience of joy, suffering, peace, and love. If we deny our hungers, we miss the mark. We form mistaken beliefs about ourselves and the world. Those mistaken beliefs generate stinking thinking, which leads us to indulge in soft addictions. We become anxious, frenetic, distracted, and unfulfilled—we live a life of Less. When we identify the deeper hungers and seek to fulfill them, we can create a life of More.

LEARNING THE LANGUAGE
OF SPIRITUAL HUNGERS

Meeting our spiritual hungers takes skill. We must recognize the hungers in the moment and make the right choices to meet them. Learning to meet our spiritual hungers is like learning a new language. It's easy to memorize vocabulary words but more difficult to speak the language fluently. Even knowing the words doesn't guarantee that we fully understand the meanings of those words. We don't gain full facility with them until we steep ourselves in their culture of origin.

Most of us are far more adept at speaking the language of our wants—our cravings for our soft addictions—than we are the more poignant language of our inner hungers. We more easily say "I want ice cream" than "I hunger for connection and to make a difference in the world."

In this chapter, you will be introduced to the vocabulary, as well as the culture, of spiritual hungers. You'll contrast that with the culture of wants and the language of soft addictions. You'll even begin to learn to translate from one language to the other. You'll become more and more adept at recognizing your spiritual hungers and meeting them in the moment, and your life of More will grow.

> ## More-sel
>
> "To desire God is the most fundamental of all human desires. It is the very root of all our quest for happiness. Even the sinner, who seeks happiness where it cannot be found, is following a blind, errant desire for God which is not aware of itself. So that, from one point of view, it is impossible not to desire God."
>
> —THOMAS MERTON

EXPERIENCE THE DIFFERENCE: SPIRITUAL
HUNGERS VS. WANTS

Spiritual hungers are the deepest longings of our hearts, a feeling of emptiness that yearns to be filled. If we had no emptiness, we might not be compelled to find God, higher purpose, or meaning. This yearning leads us to open ourselves to love, to aspire to greatness, to serve, to contribute, and to worship.

Throughout millennia, people have felt deep spiritual hunger: an urge that compelled them to build stone circles and cathedrals, to chart the movement of the heavens, to search for meaning, to explore the

rhythms of nature, to lift their heart in song, to offer thanksgiving in worship, and to believe in a force greater than themselves.

This is the universal yearning of the human heart. Beneath our differences, cultures, creeds, nationalities, belief systems, and race, runs the undercurrent of spiritual hunger that unites us all. We all hunger to be seen, to be loved, to be touched, to matter, to be part of something greater, to be one.

This spiritual hunger fuels our desire for and pursuit of More.

The Little more vs. the Big More

You know the difference between the big More of life and the little more: more stuff, gadgets, shopping, etc. But it is helpful to hone the distinctions, both in definition and how you experience them. It isn't enough to just intellectually understand the difference; you need to be able to distinguish them in the moment you are feeling them. You will be less likely to deceive yourself that some soft addiction you crave is the same as hungering for More.

For instance, we don't *hunger* for a plasma screen TV, the latest computer, or tracking Julia Roberts's every move. We *want* these things. We hunger for love, beauty, transcendence, and the opportunity to make a difference. Simply put, we *want* more. But we *hunger* for More.

More to do

What are the true yearnings of your heart? For a clue, be aware of what you think about and feel when reading about spiritual hungers. Contrast these thoughts and feelings with those you have as you read about surface wants and soft addictions.

You wouldn't think differentiating between the two would be that difficult. Unfortunately, our soft addictions blur the line between the two. We feel an urgency about both our wants and our hungers. We're convinced we can't possibly be happy or satisfied unless we possess a certain object or indulge a certain mood. At the same time, we ache for a deeper connection with others.

What's the difference?

Hungers are cravings of the soul; wants are demands of the ego. Fulfilling a hunger leads to a deep sense of satisfaction, while fulfilling a want just leads to more wanting. As our wants are satisfied, we become addictively attached to their objects and routines. We experience the short-term rush of obtaining the new car or the new gadget, but it doesn't last. When we seek the small more, we sense scarcity and feel threatened no matter how much we have. What if we can't have the object in the future or can't get more of it?

We feel anxious and don't want to let go. We are caught in the Want Cycle.

Riding the Want Cycle

Never underestimate the power of wanting. Our wants may be superficial, but they drive us powerfully. Why? Because they help us escape our deeper hungers. Precisely because our hungers are so deep, we shy away from the abyss, not knowing that true happiness waits for us in the descent. Spiritual hungers are never superficial, but their power may seem negligible compared with the drive of wants because we're so good at pushing them away.

Read the following list of wants. Note how falsely compelling they are. Say them out loud and think about what might be the real hunger that resides beneath each.

"I want an Armani suit."
"I want a BMW."
"I want that dress in the window of
    Bloomingdale's."
"I want to win the lottery."
"I want a sexy girlfriend."
"I want a rich boyfriend."
"I want space."
"I want a Krispy Kreme doughnut."
"I want to play a video game."
"I want to surf the Net."
"I want you to leave me alone and get off my back."
"I want to escape."
"I want to veg out."
"I want this bad feeling to go away."

Notice how these wants feel like "I gotta." While there is nothing wrong with these wants or with satisfying them, the intensity of them is the problem. We get caught in the Want Cycle. "I have to check my e-mail right now. I want to play a computer game immediately. I need a cup of coffee." We feel like our happiness depends on getting what we want, even though getting what we want doesn't fulfill us. The slight high or numbing sensation we get doesn't last, so we start craving or wanting again and the cycle continues.

More-sel

"Buddha's doctrine: Man suffers because of his craving to possess and keep forever things which are essentially impermanent . . . this frustration of the desire to possess is the immediate cause of suffering."
—ALAN WATTS

NAMING YOUR SPIRITUAL HUNGERS:
THE VOCABULARY OF MORE

Spiritual hungers speak to something deeper and more essential than our wants. They reflect the longings of our hearts to know that we exist, to express our essence, to experience connection with others, to make a difference or to be part of something greater than ourselves.

Hungers might be harder to name than wants, but that's only because we're not taught to look for them. Below is a list of spiritual hungers. Contrast the feel of this list with the list of the Want Cycle.

I hunger . . .

To exist
To be seen
To be heard
To be touched
To be loved
To be affirmed
To express
To experience fully
To learn
To grow
To trust
To develop
To be known
To matter
To know another human being

To be close
To feel connected
To be intimate
To love
To do what I came here on earth to do
To make a difference
To please God
To fulfill my purpose
To unfold my destiny
To feel connected to the greater whole
To be one with all
To know God

This is a general list. You can customize it and make it yours. The following examples show how people who attended one of the Wright Institute's trainings customized their hungers:

Juan: "I hunger for respect and admiration from my family, my co-workers, and people in my community."

Mickey: "I hunger for satisfaction, affirmation, and validation, both what I can bring to myself and also receive from others."

Catherine: "I yearn to have deep contact with others, to really see others, and for them to see me."

Rick: "I hunger for caring and nourishment, to see myself as a blessing, to respect myself. I hunger for joy, spontaneity, freedom of expression. I hunger to feel alive and free."

When we acknowledge our hungers, we might feel vulnerable. It can be painful or moving to express our longing for love or God or connection to the universe. Don't close your heart if pain surfaces—the pain of unfulfilled yearnings or forsaken hungers. When you open your heart to pain, you also open it to love and comfort.

> ## More-sel
>
> "Odd, the years it took to learn one simple fact: that the prize just ahead, the next job, publication, love affair, marriage always seemed to hold the key to satisfaction but never, in the longer run, sufficed."
>
> —AMANDA CROSS

ACCEPT NO SUBSTITUTES: UNDERSTANDING THE DISTINCTIONS BETWEEN WANTS AND HUNGERS

Hungers and wants often seem similar on the surface. But the distinctions matter. Let's start by looking at wants.

Wants are more visual, easier to picture, and more specific than hungers. We want very explicit things: the exact type of gadget, a certain designer's clothing, a distinct model of car, a brand of snack food, or a particular version of a computer game, or even certain people, moods, or fantasies. A want must be met exactly as it is pictured (the precise item, a particular rendition, etc.) to fully satisfy. Typically, this specificity makes wants harder to fulfill than hungers.

It's not that we shouldn't have preferences for what we

eat, buy, consume, play, think about, or work with. It's that sometimes this preference turns into an obsession that limits our freedom.

Hungers, on the other hand, are easier to fulfill because they are deeper, more essential, related to emotions, and therefore more general than wants. That means the options for fulfilling them are almost unlimited. Moreover, fulfilling any one hunger can also fulfill other hungers. By feeling loved, for instance, we may also feel known. And as we feel known, we may also feel self-respect, feel seen, and feel alive. Any spiritual hunger, once addressed, spreads a sense of fulfillment throughout our whole being.

More-sel

"If I had known what it would be like to have it all, I might have been willing to settle for less."

—LILY TOMLIN

Hungers point to a direction or a possibility. Any movement in that direction will address the hunger. Even better, the very acknowledgment of our hunger satisfies us, because we are no longer running from ourselves or hiding our deeper yearnings. We begin to understand ourselves and to find compassion. We feel and sense ourselves more deeply. We have met ourselves at a deeper level.

Unlike wants, fulfilling hungers is limited only by our own creativity. If I hunger to be loved, for example, I can call a loved one. I can re-read a heartfelt thank-you note. I can recall how someone once did something nice for me. The possibilities are limitless.

The following story about Allison shows how obsessing over a specific want can limit our opportunity for satisfaction until we admit what it was we really craved all along.

One night before the holidays, Allison was getting dressed for a casual holiday event. She had planned to wear a new, festive, comfortable outfit. When Allison looked in her closet, though, she couldn't find the matching slacks. She became consumed with finding those pants. Nothing else would do. She ripped through her closet, tossing things on the floor. She was determined that she had to wear that exact outfit. She was frantic and cursing up a storm. Without her special outfit, the evening would be filled with discomfort and worry. She had to have it.

It was only when she saw wads of clothing strewn all over the room that she realized how frenzied she was. She realized she was in the grip of her soft addictions of clothing and looking good. When Allison finally calmed down, she asked herself what she'd really been concerned about. She realized that she'd confused wanting to be seen in the "perfect" outfit with a deeper hunger to be noticed, to feel part of the holiday, and to feel loved. Once she acknowledged what she really longed for, she was able to let go of the surface want, choose another outfit, and get on with living.

> ## More-sel
>
> "We are meant to be addicted to God, but we develop secondary addictions that temporarily appear to fix our problem."
> —EDWARD M. BERCKMAN

SATISFYING YOUR SPIRITUAL HUNGERS MOMENT BY MOMENT

Indulging in a soft addiction is so reflexive, we have to be quick on the draw to shift from responding to a want to fulfilling a hunger.

Life bombards us with challenges, pressures, and tough situations all the time. Our habit is to use soft addictions to manage the emotions that result. And it happens in the blink of an eye, because that's how quickly our stinking thinking jumps in to lead us away from More and toward numbness.

It doesn't have to work that way, though. By the time we get to a soft addiction, we have actually bypassed many deeper hungers that we could have met in the moment. Satisfying your spiritual hungers doesn't require long stretches of time for quiet contemplation. Our deeper hungers can be met quickly: it is a matter of awareness and intent, not just time.

It takes practice to notice and respond to the spiritual hungers that arise moment by moment. But it can be done. Just as a tennis player can hit the ball harder by moving the racket faster, some people are more practiced in differentiating their hungers from their wants and going out to meet them. These people fulfill their hungers more rapidly.

To the extent that you can rapidly sense the difference between wants and hungers, sort through them under pressure, and go directly toward meeting your hungers, you experience More.

As I have learned to identify and respond directly to my spiritual hungers, the quality of my life has shifted dramatically. My One Decision compels me to pursue satisfying my spiritual hungers. I don't need to go through the layers of soft addictions, stinking thinking, and mistaken beliefs. Instead I can go directly to feeling connected, or loved, or to being touched. Naturally, I do give in to my soft addictions at times. But I know I have a choice and I am getting better and faster at it all the time. You'll get even more help to do this in the chapters to come, but you can start to develop your awareness of spiritual hungers and how you short-circuit them through the following exercises.

IDENTIFICATION EXERCISES: ARE YOU GOING FOR MORE OR LESS?

The more practice you have in identifying deeper hungers from wanting soft addictions, the better. This skill is definitely worth developing because your proficiency in differentiating hungers and wants can make the difference between living a life of More or a life of Less.

The following exercises are designed to help you double-check your thoughts and refine your identification skills.

1. *Identify Your Wants.* It's okay to have wants. The value is in knowing them for what they are. Have fun developing your awareness of what you want.

a. Set a timer for two minutes and make a list of your wants—from the concrete to the fanciful and from the small to the big—from coffee to reading the paper to your dream car to your salary to fantasies. Keep writing till the timer goes off.

b. Enjoy the act of wanting without having to act on your impulse. Picture a store filled with every kind of thing you have on your list. Imagine you are a small child running through the aisles saying, "I want!" Little children enjoy the act of wanting, without feeling they need to possess everything they admire. Mimic their ability to just want.

c. Pursue some of your wants. Feel free to enjoy the act of wanting to buy the car you want if you can afford it or indulge in regular television shows. There's nothing wrong with wants providing they don't start limiting or harming you or others. Your wants will have less power over you if you entertain them in moderation.

2. *Identify Your Hungers.* This is a deeper and perhaps more difficult assignment than the previous three steps so give yourself a little time and space to reflect. To help you pinpoint your hungers, do the following:

a. Review the list of hungers and place a check mark next to the ones that feel true for you. Focus on the ones that strike a chord in your heart.

b. If you haven't already, write down the hungers that resonate within you, using your own words.

c. Look at your One Decision statement. It reflects your spiritual hungers and awakens the deeper needs inside you.

d. Reflect on the More. Review the spectrum of More—more consciousness, more emotions, more connection, more spirit, and more of what fulfills spiritual hunger.

3. *Connect Your Wants and Hungers.* At this point, you should have a sense of how a specific want is merely a substitute for a deeper hunger. Take a moment and think about the hungers and wants you listed. Consider how your want-related behaviors are motivated by your hungers. Reflect on the connections between the two. I think you'll be able to complete the following sentences:

I am hungry for _____.

What I do instead is _____.

If you're having difficulty completing the sentences, consider the following examples:

I HUNGER . . .	WHAT I DO INSTEAD IS . . .
To be seen	Crack jokes
	Gossip
	Wear outrageous clothes
	Overspend on clothes
	Buy the latest gadget
	Manipulate for attention
To matter;	Buy expensive gifts for
To be important	others, outside my budget
	Be in the know—voraciously read newspapers, study data, scan the Internet obsessively for data
	Fantasize and daydream that others find me irresistible

To be touched	Act out in sexually inappropriate ways
	Compromise my standards of relationship in order to be touched
To connect	Gossip
	Overdo celebrity news
	Watch tons of television and talk about people in TV programs as if they are real acquaintances

4. *Symbolize Your Commitment to Satisfy Your Hungers.*

   a. Write your deeper hungers in a journal.

   b. Revisit your One Decision. You may want to add or shift its wording to reflect your new understanding of spiritual hungers.

   c. Now, declare your One Decision in pursuit of spiritual hungers in a symbolic way. You might want to recite it in front of the mirror, or to a trusted friend, or make a little altar with a candle to honor your One Decision.

   d. Use a lovely meal to declare your deepest hungers (e.g., "I am hungry for love"), then feed yourself (or have a loved one feed you) a delicious bite of food. It's a way to claim your deeper hungers. Try it. It may sound silly, but some who have done it said it was the most nourishing meal they ever had.

FEEDING YOUR SPIRITUAL HUNGERS

Apply your new understanding and commitment to tend to your spiritual hungers in your daily life. Try using the following exercises any time you indulge a soft addiction. The more you practice, the more adept you will become at identifying and feeding your underlying hungers. For extra practice, try the interactive template on our Web site, *www. theremustbemore.com*.

1. *Identify hungers.* Ask yourself:

What was I truly hungry for in the moment?

What might have been different if I had been in touch with my deeper hungers instead of just my surface wants?

2. *Create positive thoughts.* While leading a pilgrimage to Israel, I discovered another way to respond to spiritual hungers by creating positive thoughts to replace the stinking thoughts. A group of us had done meaningful spiritual work on the shores of the Sea of Galilee. Deeply inspired by the words of the beatitudes and with our hearts freshly opened, we began to see the positive intention beneath each other's stinking thinking and soft addiction routines. We delivered a form of blessing to one another to reflect this new, loving "frame" for each person. Here are some examples:

> ## More to do
>
> ---
>
> **Be a Renegade Blesser.** Create a blessing for a friend, coworker, or loved one. Write it on a sticky note and put it on their computer; hide a note in their briefcase; send it in an e-mail; or even write it in frosting on a big cookie.

Blessed is she who hungers to be heard, for she shall express the sounds of her heart.

Blessed is he who hungers to be known, for he shall make his mark upon the earth in the service of all.

Blessed is he who pursues More in his life, for he shall discover the treasures of the universe.

Blessed is she who feels deeply, for she will know the richness of her heart.

Blessed is he who feels alone on his path, for through his journey he will know both himself and the companionship of spirit.

Do the same for yourself. Write a blessing for yourself to address your spiritual hunger.

HUNGER FOR A SENSE OF DEEP CONNECTION

The benefits of focusing on hungers will show up everywhere—including your relationships. So often we make the mistake of sharing only our surface wants. As a result, we end up with partners who share our soft addictions instead of our spiritual hungers! But when we share our hungers with another person, we attain true intimacy, a deep sharing of soul to soul.

I can tell the difference just in a conversation with my husband. When Bob and I talk, it is very nourishing because we express our spiritual hungers and deeper yearnings directly. We don't spend the bulk of our time talking about our surface wants or our soft addictions. Instead of discussing television programs or celebrity news or gossip, we share what matters most to us with love, truth, lightness, humor, and emotion. To be sure, we still have our soft addictions and off moments. But we know how to reorient to our deeper hungers and desires.

Don't wait until you already know someone well to connect through deeper hungers rather than wants. You'll miss out on great possibilities for connection. When I was leading a pilgrimage in France, we had arranged to meet and learn about the Jerusalem monks, an urban coeducational order, in the heart of Paris. There we met Sister Edith, whose first words to us were, "All my life I have been searching for God." We loved the simplicity of her statement and how it directly revealed a universal hunger. We knew so much about her from those words. The ensuing conversation was blissfully uplifting. There was no small talk or beating around the bush. She established a

> ## More to do
>
> Read through the singles ads in your newspaper. How many of them reflect surface wants? How many reflect spiritual hungers?

powerful connection both with us and with herself when she articulated her hunger.

Knowing your spiritual hungers and differentiating them from your soft addictions is an important skill in living More. In the next chapter, you will develop a vision of a life in which you fulfill your spiritual hungers and implement your One Decision. As you'll discover, we all are visionaries at heart.

8.

DEVELOPING A VISION

"A vision without a task is but a dream,
a task without a vision is drudgery, a vision and
a task are the hope of the world."
—from a church in Sussex, England, c. 1730

By this point, you have probably realized that a life of More is not just about quitting soft addictions. In fact, addressing soft addictions isn't the real focus—meeting your spiritual hungers is the key. Just getting rid of a substance or an activity doesn't solve anything. Releasing one soft addiction often just makes space for another. Our deeper hungers persist because they're still unfulfilled. This is the point where the power of vision comes into play. Inspiring and uplifting, your vision can help you resist the allure of your soft addictions. Your vision will guide and propel you to a life of More.

Your vision reflects what is really important to you, what matters deep in your heart. Vision gives you the momentum to move through the barriers of your soft addictions. Your deeper yearnings provide fuel to power your vision. Mahatma Gandhi hungered for connection, justice, and unity. These hungers defined his vision and carried him through untold barriers toward his dream of a unified, free India. Similarly, we are still moving toward the vision of Martin Luther King, Jr., fueled by his passion for justice, equality, and love.

More-sel

"I have a dream that one day this nation will rise up and live out the true meaning of its creed, 'We hold these truths to be self-evident, that all men are created equal.' This is our hope . . . With this faith we will be able to work together, to pray together, to struggle together, to go to jail together, to stand up for freedom together, knowing that we will be free one day . . ."

—MARTIN LUTHER KING, JR.

We usually spend more time planning and visualizing our soft addiction routines than imagining the possibilities of fulfilling our heart's desires. We are often more adept at fantasizing and filling wants than envisioning and filling deeper hungers. A vision helps us cultivate our capacity to see beyond the surface to what could be.

Suzanne had a picture of what she wanted, but not a vision of what she hungered for. As a gregarious cosmetics representative, she had plenty of engaging contact with women, but she craved men's attention. She imagined herself escorted by the hunkiest hunks and courted by royalty. She dreamt of having gourmet meals, armloads of flowers, and presents from her favorite designer store. Suzanne had planned her wedding hundreds of times yet had never been engaged. She flirted outrageously, dressed provocatively, couldn't seem to stop herself from making eyes at every guy, and depended upon men's attention to give her ego a boost. Suzanne showed little discrimination in whom she dated. She just liked being with men. Without a man around, she felt empty and worthless.

Suzanne began learning the skills of this book and slowly realized: "Dating, getting a man's attention, and having only short-lived relationships have become soft addictions for me. I thought that if men gave me expensive gifts, it meant I was valuable. For a long time, I've relied on men to make me feel good about myself. I haven't imagined feeling good about myself on my own. I have glimmers but it feels unreal—not concrete. I have been living in fantasies without a vision of a fulfilling life as a strong woman."

With this understanding, Suzanne began building her vision and then drafted a plan for enacting it. She recognized her deeper hunger to be seen and loved. She made her One Decision and decided to pursue fulfilling her spiritual hungers: "I am a multifaceted woman I respect, and I trust that I am loved. I draw my security from my inner resources, my capacities, my relationship with spirit." Her Vision is: "I express myself fully and honestly. I am recognized, acknowledged, and appreciated by myself and the world around me. Strong and independent, I support myself financially and emotionally. I respect myself and am well treated by myself and others. I date men whom I respect and who respect me."

Suzanne felt strengthened by holding a strong image of herself as an independent woman who feels comfortable without a relationship. Not only did she change her dress to adopt a more conservative tone, she found new strength in herself rather than depending on others to give it to her. She also began to draw on the support of her circle of women friends. With her Vision as a beacon before her, Suzanne aligned her life following it. She developed an action plan to build the confidence and skills to live her Vision. She enrolled in courses and learning laboratories at the Wright Institute and participated in assignments to improve her relationship with herself and with men.

WHAT IS VISION?

With vision, you see more clearly how to achieve the More you seek. Vision is the projection into the future of a spiritually fulfilled life based on your One Decision and intent to live the More. It is a picture of your One Decision in action. Vision may shift with the evolving changes in your life, but its intent remains constant.

Vision differs from goal setting. A goal is measurable with a specific time, space, or quantity. You will create a Formula for More with goals to help you implement your vision in the next chapter. But Vision is the starting place. For instance, a vision related to your body might be: *I am lithe and flexible. I enjoy being in my body*. Your goal, then, might be to be able touch your toes within a month's time. Your specific action might be to take a yoga class.

What We See Is What We Get

Vision guides all our lives. Whether you know it or not, your life has been formed by some sort of vision, positive or negative. Sadly, it is too often an expression of our negative thinking, unconscious belief systems, and poor self-esteem.

A positive vision helps us avoid cycling through limiting self-fulfilling prophecies driven by unconscious beliefs. Often we're not even conscious of this cycle. For instance, if we believe that we cannot fulfill our spiritual hungers, then we unconsciously act in a way that confirms and reinforces that belief.

Peter holds an unconscious belief that things in his life are never going to be good for him. He lives in fear, waiting for something bad to happen; he imagines bad endings to conversations and being rejected. Peter repeatedly sees himself in disastrous situations, humiliating outcomes, and unsatisfying results. His vision is a negative vision, based on false beliefs and an addiction to pessimistic moods. His mind is more focused on planning problems than developing solutions. Feeling discouraged and hopeless, Peter overindulges by watching television late into the night, eating sugary snack foods, and wallowing in his pessimistic moods. His addictive routine feeds his negative worldview and vice versa. This cycle keeps him from acting in positive ways. He consistently concludes, "See, I knew nothing good could ever happen to me."

With a positive vision, Peter can create a picture of fulfilling his spiritual hunger rather than indulging his addictions. Even if his unconscious mind still holds self-defeating beliefs about himself, he can act in accordance with his new positive Vision. Orienting to his Vision helps him to change his actions, challenges his faulty belief systems, and compels him to overcome his fear.

Where Visions Come From . . . and How to Access That Place

Vision is not something available only to a select few. I have worked with hundreds of people who, on the surface, don't seem like visionaries. Yet they've developed visions and made them come true. I am constantly inspired by the fact that we can all discover the uplifting, loving dreams flowing inside each one of us when we listen to our hearts, rise above our soft addictions, and align to the One Decision.

Sarah came to the Institute because she wanted to lose weight. When I asked her why, she looked at me like I was crazy, saying, "Isn't it obvious?"

More to do

Make a list of visionaries throughout history, like Walt Disney, Hildegard von Bingen, and Martin Luther King, Jr. What do they have in common?

Not to me it wasn't. While certainly not model thin, Sarah was attractive, well groomed, and artfully dressed. She was a success in the competitive world of advertising. Why would she be focused on her weight? I asked her questions to assess her negative and positive visions: What is it that you hope losing weight will give to you? How do you want to feel about your body? How do you want to relate to your body? What do you want to use your body for? What would you feel like?

Sarah investigated these questions and her soft addictions. The answers she found allowed her to articulate her higher Vision—one that revolved around physical health and creativity, not just thinness. She talked about how she saw herself completely relaxed with her appearance. She wanted the grace and physical expressiveness of a dancer. This is the Vision she formulated: "I am sensuous and supple and surround myself with sumptuous self-care."

Along with her One Decision, Sarah articulated an inspiring Vision of More, not just a diet to stick to and a problem to solve. This Vision made it worthwhile to shift her routines.

> ### More to do
>
> Be inspired by the visionary, and my hero, Jacques Lusseryan. Read *And There Was Light* for a deeply moving, challenging, exhilarating example of a life of More.

DESIGNING YOUR LIFE:
CREATING YOUR VISION OF MORE

Now it's time for you to create your Vision. The following exercises are designed to help you unleash your Vision. Allow yourself to dream a life of More where you fulfill your spiritual hungers, guided by your One Decision.

Your Designer Life

Imagine you have just arrived on this planet. You can review and choose from all ways of being in all walks of life to design your life any way you want. What activities, feelings, and experiences will you choose? What values will you select to guide you and how will you incorporate them? If you proactively designed your life, what would it look like?

Most likely, you wouldn't design a life based on your surface wants. You wouldn't actually plan on watching nineteen hours of television a week. You wouldn't stipulate twelve hours of daydreaming weekly or insist you really need to surf the Internet until your eyes water and your brain becomes bleary. Compulsive shopping, worry, and self-pity routines wouldn't be high on your list, either.

What we all desire is a life following our highest values, pursuing and satisfying our spiritual hungers. Think about how you would design your ideal life. What would you put into this ideal life design? Jot down your ideas, if you wish. You'll find them useful when you create your Vision.

Vision Do's and Don'ts

You can taste, feel, hear, and see a powerful Vision. Wording it in the present tense gives it the most power because you imagine yourself doing, not planning. Remember, it is not a reaction to a particular problem or situation. The following Do's and Don'ts will help you create a strong Vision:

DO	DON'T
Do fulfill your spiritual hungers	Don't just feed your surface wants
Do have a proactive vision	Don't settle for a reactive vision

DO	DON'T
Do feed your soul	Don't just cater to your ego
Do write your Vision in present tense	Don't write it in the future tense
Do create a Vision that deepens your life experience	Don't fantasize an escape from life
Do picture your One Decision in action	Don't picture your soft addictions in action
Do inspire yourself	Don't numb yourself
Do picture how you will feel, what will be, what your life will be	Don't settle for a vague wish
Do go for the More	Don't go for more stuff
Do be sure it is yourself you please	Don't worry about pleasing others
Do keep your wording positive and affirmative	Don't use "not" in your vision
Do envision More	Don't limit your possibilities

CRAFTING YOUR VISION

Create a truly holistic Vision that encompasses who you are in all aspects of your being. Picture yourself living your One Decision and fulfilling your spiritual hungers to create a life of More.

You can develop an overall vision for your life, or you can start by designing visions for specific aspects of your life. You may find it helpful to use the areas of life that we use at the Institute, drawn from Bob Wright's Comprehensive Model of Human Growth and Development, as you'll see below. Don't feel that you need to compose a vision for every area of your life. Pick the areas that seem most important to you right now, or the ones you are most anxious to change.

Let yourself flow and dream. What would you do? What would you feel like? Imagine the quality of your experience.

To get you started, here are a range of examples from our students' visions for various areas of life. Let them inspire you to create your own.

My Body: My body is pain-free, and I feel good about it. I move with grace and I am strong. I have both muscles and feminine curves. I lovingly nourish my body and enjoy it.

My Self: I feel self-confident, and I treat myself with respect. I think in positive ways that help me succeed

More alert

Potential obstacles to developing your Vision:

Being embarrassed about your deeper hungers
Listening only to your head and not your heart
Confusing vision with vague wishes, such as "I want to be happy"
Mistaking escapist fantasies for the potential realities of Vision
Being afraid of change

in relationships and work. I encourage myself and do not allow guilt or shame to hold me back. I am continually learning and growing and deepening my capacity to love myself and others.

My Family: My family is a source of strength, solace, and support. We value truth and genuineness. I challenge and support them to be their best and they do the same for me. We move through conflict honestly and openly because we value each other's experience.

With Others: I count on my friends and they can count on me. We tell the truth, share our feelings, and expect a lot from one another. Our lives are adventures of mutual support and celebration as we encourage each other to our highest.

My Work: I am a leader in my field, an excellent manager and salesperson. I am constantly learning, growing, and improving in my work, and supporting those around me to grow and be their best. I create value and serve: I am proud that those I supervise are valuable workers.

My Society: I contribute my time, energy, and gifts to people and causes that matter to me. I bring truth, aliveness, engagement, and service to my communities. I value the earth and volunteer at prairie restoration projects.

My Spirituality: I am a spiritual man. I am engaged in an active journey of faith. I focus on spirit throughout my day, to learn to live more sacredly. I follow a path of truth and love even in difficult times, supported by my faith and friends.

Overall Vision: Life is a great adventure of growing and learning and I live it fully. I care deeply about the world around me and am a "net giver" in all that I do.

My Vision of More

Jot down your Vision. Don't worry about making it perfect. The very act of imagining your life of More will serve you. Once you have written something, go back to the Do's and Don'ts and make sure that you have followed these guidelines. Use the following questions to spark your imagination.

My One Decision: What was your One Decision? (You may want to refer to Chapter 3 as a reminder.)

_____

_____

_____

_____

_____

My Spiritual Hungers: What are your spiritual hungers, your deeper yearnings? Let them inspire your Vision. How would you live your life if you were oriented toward fulfilling your spiritual hungers in each of the following areas of life?

_____

_____

_____

_____

_____

My Body: Think about your relationship with your body. Do you hunger for touch, to know you exist, to connect? What would your ideal relationship with your body look like? How do you feel about your body now and what would you like to be different? Most of us have a narrow idea of the potential in our relationship to our body, defined by surface-oriented media. Picture yourself in a healthy relationship with your body. Really stretch for the exquisite richness of sensation, fullness of breath, and experience of aliveness.

_____

_____

_____

_____

_____

My Self: How do you want to feel about yourself? What deeper hungers do you wish to fulfill: To know you exist? To learn and grow, to develop, etc.? What is your vision for your self-development, self-esteem, and self-respect? Picture what it might be like to have your feelings and emotions more available. Imagine a relationship with yourself that is satisfying. What might that look like? Consider the possibility of rich awareness, deep compassion, and support for your well-being, and reach for it in your vision.

_____

_____

_____

_____

_____

My Family: How do you envision your relationship with your family of origin and your family of choice? What hungers do you picture fulfilling—to be affirmed, to connect, to be heard, etc.? What would be different with your family? What do you picture when you dream about your ideal family state?

_____

_____

_____

_____

_____

With Others: What hungers do you want to meet with others—to be affirmed, to be respected, to connect? What do you want from your relationships with friends, coworkers, acquaintances, neighbors, etc.? What would your contact with these people look like? What would you do that you are not currently doing?

_____

_____

_____

_____

_____

My Work and Play: What hungers do you long to meet at work—to express, to be seen and valued, to develop your talents? What do you hunger for in playtime? Envision recreation that refreshes you. Imagine how you could weave work and play together in your workday. How would your days look when defined by this vision?

_____

_____

_____

_____

_____

My Society: What do you hunger for in your relationship to society at large—to make a difference, to contribute, to matter and have an impact on your community? What is important to you? How would you integrate your principles and values into your public life? How would your days be different?

_____

_____

_____

_____

_____

My Spirituality: What do you hunger for in the realm of spirituality—to feel connected to something greater than yourself, to feel part of the whole? How might you feel if you were more satisfied in this area of your life? What might you do differently or shift in your daily routine? What if your spirituality infused all aspects of your life? How could the different areas of your life fit together synergistically to bring you spiritual fulfillment?

_____

_____

_____

_____

_____

_____

Other Areas: Is there another area of your life that these don't cover? Write it here and envision satisfaction and fulfillment in this area as well.

_____

_____

_____

_____

_____

My Overall Vision: Given your answers above, what does your life look like as you live according to your One Decision? Picture a life that meets your spiritual hunger.

_____

_____

_____

_____

_____

Inspire Yourself with Your Vision

Do you feel inspired by reading what you've written? If so, you know you have captured the essence of your Vision.

Now do something with your Vision. Share it with a friend. Make it into a screen saver on your computer. Embroider it on a quilt. Put a note on your bathroom mirror. You need to make contact with it again and again. Use it to inspire you and to guide your actions. Post it on a wall. Review it so that it continues to grow and feed you. Make a creative collage that represents your Vision. Light a candle and pray over it. Write it in your journal.

Put a notice in your calendar to review it daily for one week, then weekly (at least) after that. Write your Vision in your file on our Web site, *www.theremustbemore.com,* and we'll send it to you at intervals you request. After one year, review and revise it.

Don't let this exercise overwhelm you. Even just thinking about it can be energizing. While you can spend as much time on it as you want, you can write a vision for each area of life in a minute or two. Many have completed visions for all areas of their life in ten to fifteen minutes. It also can help to do this with a friend, interviewing each other and recording each other's responses. (It's great to do on a date!) Remember, you can change your Vision at any time, so don't feel every word has to be perfect now. Experiment and see how you feel about your results. If it feels right to you, it probably is.

More to do

Write a letter to yourself, stating your Vision. Give it to a friend and ask him or her to mail it to you in a year, accompanied by a note from that person asking: How are you living your Vision?

Creating a vision is empowering, but implementing it will truly change your life. In the next chapter, you'll find the tools necessary to turn your Vision into daily action, as aided by a wonderfully simple, easy-to-use concept called The Math of More.

9.

THE MATH OF MORE: ADDING AND SUBTRACTING TO ACHIEVE YOUR VISION

"Dismiss what insults your soul and your very flesh will become a great poem."

—WALT WHITMAN

Powered by your One Decision, a deceptively simple formula generates the More: Add things that enhance your Vision and subtract things that take away from it.

In this new math, adding actually subtracts and subtracting adds. Adding real nourishment to your life naturally subtracts your soft addictions, literally pushing them out of the way. And when you subtract your soft addictions, you automatically add more time, resources, and consciousness to pursue the More.

You'll learn to add substance to your life, not fill your life with substances. In short, you will discover the Formula for More.

LEARNING THE NEW MATH

Living according to the Math of More makes our dreams come true. The Math lets you generate your own formula for

More, an action plan to realize your Vision. Most people think that when they have a bad habit, they should just use their willpower and stop it. Think of all the people who have lost weight only to gain it again, or those who replace one addiction like smoking with another like overeating. Merely getting rid of a soft addiction doesn't lead to a life of More. Addressing your deeper hungers does. The Math of More helps you clarify what to add to your life to meet these hungers. When you add to your life, you are less likely to replace one addiction with another.

Learning to Add

While you may need to curb some of your soft addictions and get rid of others, the main focus in the Math of More is to add nourishing things to your life. When you add more reading, socializing, or getting together with friends, you'll watch TV less. If you usually gossip at work, talking about yourself instead of others will shift the focus. Many more examples of these activities will be found later in this chapter.

Learning to Subtract

As we've said, in the Math of More, subtracting actually adds. Subtracting means decreasing the percentage of time, money, resources, and energy tied up with soft addiction routines. Subtracting does not necessarily mean eliminating something completely or immediately. You don't need to subtract down to zero; just reducing the frequency, duration, or intensity of a behavior works to create More.

THE FORMULA FOR MORE

The Formula for More is simple:

Life + Spiritual Nourishment – Soft Addictions = The More

The skills you have been learning throughout this book feed the formula by giving you ideas for each element of the equation. To see the process in action, let's look at Tyler's approach to living his Vision using the Math of More. You can use this example when you create your own formula for More at the end of the chapter.

Tyler wanted More out of life, but his military background didn't provide him with tools to get the warmth and connection he hungered for. Growing up on an army base, the fourth of six children, he learned early on the importance of hard work and discipline. His adult life became a series of non-nourishing yet practical routines. He worked out too much, sometimes to the point of injury. He ate sparsely, like he was always rationing. He dutifully upheld all of his responsibilities but took little pleasure in them. While he valued hard work, his career success meant little to him. He didn't really enjoy his achievements.

> # More-sel
>
> "I merely took the energy it takes to pout and wrote some blues."
>
> —DUKE ELLINGTON

Underneath, Tyler was a vital, energetic man, but on the surface all you could see was his stoic veneer. He hungered for more human connection, flexibility, and spontaneity. He yearned to use his military training for higher purposes and to apply his fierceness to causes that mattered to him.

Tyler began his Formula for More by reviewing his One Decision and his overall Vision. Next, Tyler wrote down the soft addictions that were in the way of achieving his Vision and the spiritual hungers that he most wanted to address. Then, Tyler applied the Math of More to implement his Vision. He developed long-term goals and action steps, the concrete activities that would get him to his goals. For both goals and action steps, he planned what he would add to his life and what he would subtract.

Tyler's Formula for More

My One Decision

I commit to a life of truth—ruthless, loving truth. I will not hide from life—I will live it fully and consciously. I am deeply committed to manifesting gratitude and joy in everything I do. I pursue love and connection.

My Vision

I am a robust and vital man, a man of consequence in my world. I live strongly and fiercely, giving freely of myself. I am alive and engaged, learning and growing with excitement, constantly orienting toward higher principles and my One Decision.

My Soft Addictions

> Mood addiction in the form of gloomy thoughts
> Solitary excessive workouts and weight training
> Sparse, utilitarian meals
> Caffeine and sugary drinks
> Television, especially late-night viewing of violent
>   action shows

My Spiritual Hungers

> To be affirmed and acknowledged
> To matter

My Additions

My Goals

Increase nourishing, sustaining meals by 50%

Add more playing: softball, biking, playing at the park with my daughter, etc., at least once a week

Increase flexibility by working out and experimenting with other ways to be in my body (Tai Chi, Aikido, yoga, etc.) at least twice a week

Provide intellectual stimulation and alternative entertainment by reading at least one good book a month

Increase self-respect by increasing self-care, acknowledging my successes, seeking positive feedback from others, and bragging at least once a week

Generate my own excitement and adventure instead of watching it on television by taking a risk a week and stretching myself

My Action Steps

First three weeks:
Enjoy a three-course dinner once a week with my wife

Get bike tuned up

Go to bookstore

Take a class in Aikido or Tai Chi

Next three weeks:
Begin reading a book

Go on a bike ride

Ask my wife to tell me what she admires about me

Keep an acknowledgment journal to track my successes and the positive things others say about me

Watch a "chick flick" with my wife (rather than another violent adventure movie) and try to find some redeeming value in it

My *Subtractions*

My Goals

Decrease soft drinks by 50%

Limit workouts to one hour, and three times a week

Limit television viewing to no more than two hours a night

My Action Steps

First three weeks:
Drink two caffeinated sodas per day instead of four to six

Work out six times per week instead of seven

Move television out of the bedroom

Next three weeks:
Drink one caffeinated soda per day

Work out five times per week

Enjoy one night per week without TV

ADDING UP TO A LIFE OF MORE

You don't have to invent a life of More from scratch. In the rest of this chapter, you will learn the kinds of things you can add and subtract: activities of self-care and nourishment, self-expression and personal development, self-realization and spirituality. Think about what you'd like to add to *your* life as you read.

The ideas in this chapter offer inspiration but not a prescription. This is about discovering what works for you and brings your Vision closer to fruition. It is not about following a recipe, but about following your heart. Dream about possibilities for your life as you discover the many ways to care for, develop, and discover your self.

ADD SELF-CARE AND NOURISHMENT

Self-care means anything that maintains or feeds your body, soul, mind, and spirit and contributes to creating More in life. Self-care is foundational. It starts with becoming aware of your feelings, needs, and hungers. It can include maintaining clean and neat surroundings, giving more hugs, being spontaneous, dancing, adhering to financial discipline, being organized, stimulating your intellect. We often confuse soft addictions and self-care. True self-care satisfies our hungers, not our wants. A conscious renewal break is very different from indulging soft addictions. Morgan's story illustrates the difference.

Morgan is a hardworking advertising executive. Always impeccably dressed and immaculately groomed, she strived to make a good impression. Driven to succeed, she put in long hours at work and networked constantly. She tended to be wound up and would be abrupt in her communications— curt, terse, and to the point. Getting ahead was important to her. Her father had a history of reversals of fortune, declaring bankruptcy more than once. She vowed early in her life that she would not be like him, and would have not only financial security but abundance.

If she took time for herself just to be, or even to go to the art museum (which she loved), Morgan felt guilty, like she was goofing off. After skipping breakfast, she usually ate her lunch while working at her desk. She kept her finances and her house in order and scheduled haircuts, facials, and massages as a regular regimen. But she treated herself like she was a car that needed regular maintenance, not a woman deserving of loving self-care.

Morgan came to the Institute to develop more intimate relationships in her life. She discovered that she needed to become intimate with herself first. Through her courses and the support of other students, she learned to treat herself as someone worthy and special. She applied her ability to be disciplined to real self-care. She scheduled two breaks during each business day where she would take a walk or call a friend and just chat. Morgan packed picnics for herself and took them to the park instead of eating at her desk. On Friday night, she was more likely to be at the opening of an art gallery in town than catching up at the office. Surprisingly, her work benefited as she found she had more energy and became more productive and more creative from the stimulation she received from her self-care. She began to enjoy her free moments and used them to restore herself. She scheduled long weekend vacations and went to cities with great art museums. She allowed herself more nourishment, and a sense of peace pervaded her life.

The following are possibilities to help you increase your self-care. Consider building routines of self-care that increase your baseline of nurturance.

Add Nourishment and Maintenance

You may not be as disciplined as Morgan and may need to add regular self-care routines like exercise, regular massages, or dates with your spouse. Decide the frequency, schedule them for the year, and put them on your calendar. Then, do not cancel one without rescheduling it. Look for routines to support your physical, financial, and emotional health—from exercise and healthy eating to financial integrity and vacations.

Morgan needed to experience nourishment, not just go through the motions. You can take a moment to find nourishment in your daily rituals, whether it's purposeful stretching when you awaken, caressing your face as you wash in the morning, or lovingly rubbing lotion into your skin rather than slapping it on. Let your daily bath or shower be a time of sensory indulgence. Nourish yourself during the day with conscious breathing, stretch breaks, or calls to friends. Make mealtimes nourishing for your body and soul by eating lunch on a park bench instead of at your desk. Read something inspirational, jot in a journal, lunch by a favorite tree, write a poem, walk in the park, meditate, take a ten-minute nap, or take in a museum exhibit. Tuck yourself in at night rather than flopping into bed.

Consciously chosen self-care is not indulgent or extraneous. It sustains you in your Vision. You finish your day energized rather than drained. It creates a baseline for living a life of More.

Add Space and Time to Be and Feel

Adding some quiet moments to your day helps you be more comfortable with yourself and less likely to mindlessly fill time alone. When you are with yourself quietly, you face your feelings rather than fleeing from them via a soft addiction.

Most of us don't have much experience being with ourselves in this way. To just "be" is different from hanging out in unconsciousness or indulging a soft addiction routine. It allows our unconscious impulses and thoughts to rise to the surface. This sensation can be frightening or unsettling when we are not used to it or have spent years pushing this repressed part of ourselves away. It is often difficult to feel valuable when you are just "being" instead of doing, even if the doing was indulging in a soft addiction.

Morgan called the alone, end-of-day moments "squirrelly windows of time." She felt uneasy slowing down and being in an intensely personal state. At the fringes of her consciousness, she sensed the tumult of unresolved feelings, undone tasks, and self-judgments she had kept at bay. She didn't want them to surface, so she used soft addiction routines as a shield. She called up friends to go shopping, made tennis dates, and talked for hours on the phone about other people's problems to avoid being figuratively and literally alone.

Luckily, she identified her discomfort, realizing she had trouble being with herself. She learned to talk herself through it, telling herself that she might feel uncomfortable for a few minutes, but it was worth it to deepen her relationship with herself. In fact, Morgan developed an ability to check in with herself on an ongoing basis to see how she felt and to determine what she needed in the moment. She began to hunger for her private space to discover herself, rather than running away from herself. This ability allowed her to follow the dictates of her heart rather than her habits.

Spend at least a few minutes being quiet every day. Just sit still, meditate, pray, or look out the window. If you find silent stillness difficult, gradually increase your time with yourself. Eventually, this practice may add up to a larger meditation or prayer discipline, or taking a Sabbath day a week.

> ## More to do
>
> Stop. Right now. Take a deep breath. Stretch. Close your eyes. Spend a brief moment with yourself right this minute. Aahhhh.

Whether you add ten minutes of quiet time or many hours, you will learn to appreciate the empty space inside and allow it to fill with spirit instead of stuff.

ADD SELF-EXPRESSION AND
SELF-DEVELOPMENT

While self-care is foundational, self-expression and self-development are more advanced ways we can make positive additions to our formula. Developing and expressing ourselves means we practice positive ways of being, we develop and share our gifts and talents, and we honor and express our feelings and assert our will. We generate meaning by stepping into our fullest potential, by remembering the truest essence of who we are, and by expressing it with, to, and for others.

As Morgan continued her journey to More, she felt like she was becoming more herself and becoming more of a multi-dimensional woman. Treating herself to more loving self-care, she was feeling more worthy and secure. Previously somewhat humorless, she began to develop a healthy acceptance of herself, and she unveiled a sly, sardonic sense of humor. Coming from this well-groomed, straight-postured woman, it was charmingly disarming. Before, revealing her humor had felt too intimate to her, and now it felt refreshing and freeing. Where once she feared that self-acceptance would mean indulgence, she has discovered that it has really caused her to feel less anxiety. She turned less to soft addictions and more to positive modes of expression.

Morgan's artistic ability had been previously expressed in her advertising work, but she began to add other forms of creative expression. She enrolled in a printmaking class and journaled and wrote poetry like she used to in college. She even read one of her poems at an open-mike poetry evening at the local coffeehouse. At work, she remains assertive yet creates deeper contact with people. Her organizational skills are now being shared with others. She even began writing poetic e-mail memos and joking with her division president about problems at work. He told her that he was feeling comfortable with her for the first time and asked her to head up the quality of life task force. Not only was her quality of life improving, but she would also help others to that end.

Add Developing and Sharing Your Gifts and Talents

We all have undeveloped gifts, talents, and skills. Our Vision moves closer to reality when we nurture and develop these special attributes. Whatever wonderful picture you have of yourself in the future, it emerges from these authentic gifts and not from inauthentic soft addictions. Sharing your gifts with the world is something you can do no matter the level of your gift development, whether beginner or master. For example, you don't have to be a concert pianist to share your piano playing with friends, at a nursing home, or for your own enjoyment. Perhaps you are a good listener, play a mean game of tennis, bake great chocolate chip cookies, or can change the oil in any car. Maybe you are a great love-letter writer, picture hanger, computer whiz, or whirlwind house cleaner. Honor your gift and be generous with it, no matter what it is.

Add Ability to Be with Feelings

The more you engage with your emotions, the less you will indulge your soft addictions. Whatever your Vision is, conscious, responsible expression of your feelings draws you to it. Your emotions hold immense clues about your concerns and hungers. If you learn to be with yourself and your feelings, you learn to draw on the wisdom of your heart. Your awareness of hurt will lead you to comfort; your anger will lead to greater effectiveness; and all of your emotions will lead to greater fulfillment. Give yourself permission to feel.

Add Creative Expression and Humor

Soft addictions are often reactive: you react to the discomfort of a feeling or to an event that stirs feelings you haven't even identified. Conversely, creative self-expression is pro-active: you put something forward of your own accord.

Creativity does not just spring from artists, musicians, and craftspersons. We can all create in every mode of expression. Expressing yourself through conversation, work, song, decorating, making a great dish for dinner, or by voicing your opinion are just some of the possibilities. Anything that creates something new and expresses an inner urge is creative. The more you create and express, the more alive you feel and the less you will numb yourself.

If you see the humor in your behavior, you can look at yourself with a more compassionate, objective perspective. Humor tends to diminish your perfectionism, allowing you to feel more free to create and take risks. Maintaining a sense of humor about yourself helps you fearlessly examine soft addictions and admit some of the nutty things you do. You can laugh about the hours spent scanning the papers for the best deals on jogging shoes or about how you drift into daydreams while people are talking to you. Adding a sense of humor helps you to feel genuine delight and get naturally "high" so you don't depend on soft addictions for an artificial buzz. More consciousness and awareness means more creativity, spontaneity, and flow—all of which help you experience more natural joy and delight.

More to do

Host a "Foible Fest" with your friends. Share your silliest moments.

ADD SELF-REALIZATION AND SPIRITUALITY

Whereas self-expression finds its outlet in creative activity, self-realization deals with our being, rather than our doing. It is consciousness rather than activity. It is an awareness of our unity with the transcendent. It means identifying your life purpose, fostering beauty, love, aliveness, consciousness, nourishment, gratitude, and compassion. You wake up to the life around you and begin to live the transcendent in your daily life. Spirituality becomes an ever-growing part of your life. Self-realization means aligning with our highest selves. Morgan discovered such a sense of transcendence in a most unlikely place.

Who would have thought that a hard-driving advertising executive would experience mystical union in a business meeting, but that is exactly what happened to Morgan. In the middle of a presentation, she looked around the room and suddenly comprehended that everyone wanted the best for her. Her heart opened and she felt a deep caring for everyone in the room. She realized that she was not only presenting a marketing plan but also supporting the overall spiritual development of herself and everyone in the room. It was as if all were gathered to fulfill a higher purpose far beyond the presentation.

While this might seem to be a flight of fancy, Morgan began changing the nature of her advertising design out of this understanding. Guided by clear purpose and spiritual perspectives, Morgan sought to add an inspirational, uplifting element in every advertisement that honored the highest self in each of us.

Upon hearing of an illness or seeing someone struggle or suffer, she found herself automatically saying brief prayers at work. She felt that her life of faith was deepening as she moved into increasingly vulnerable and meaningful conversations with coworkers. She became intensely curious about everyone's spiritual life, and by asking others about their spiritual practices, she felt that she was learning and expanding her own. She had never thought of herself as particularly conscious or compassionate until one day when her secretary asked her what she had been doing to become so caring and aware of those around her. Morgan began to find everything she did fueled by the excitement and challenge of living to her highest potential every day, in every way.

Add Being Awake, Alive, and Spiritually Nourished

Morgan realized that adding consciousness and awareness to life allows us to be more present and available and to bring ourselves to every moment. Increased consciousness supported by spiritual nourishment allows us to emerge from the fog and feel life coursing through us and around us.

Adding consciousness and boosting aliveness can be as easy as reminding yourself to wake up and pay attention, reading a book on the power of presence, or taking a dance, yoga, or meditation class. Spiritual nourishment boosts and maintains our baseline of consciousness and aliveness. Spiritual nourishment is akin to the new leaf pushing the old leaf—the soft addiction–related behaviors—off the limb.

A spiritually nourishing moment doesn't need to take time. It's hugging a friend, capturing a snowflake on your tongue, expressing feelings, walking in the park, meditating, or pouring love from heart to heart as we gaze into the eyes of our beloved. True spirituality transcends our traditional religious views and beliefs. It's a sacredness found in everyday moments and experiencing all of life as a sacred journey.

Add Beauty and Inspiration

Adding beauty and inspiration to your life nourishes your spirit. Beauty has a power to move you and make you feel better about yourself. A flower at your breakfast table, a photo of your beloved on your desk, or a beautiful screen saver lifts our spirit. Organization itself possesses a powerful beauty. Creating clean, uncluttered spaces and orderliness soothes the spirit and helps you relax. Beauty in all its forms creates a powerful doorway through which inspiration and creativity can enter.

Inspiration includes anything that touches your heart or moves your soul, such as poetry, music, stories of courage, love notes, and sacred texts. Always keep something inspirational on hand so you have instant access during transition times (such as the end of the workday) or when tempted by your soft addiction routines.

Inspiration can be simple and portable—a small booklet in your purse, an uplifting CD, or a quote or photo in your wallet. I keep a "God bag" packed with a variety of ever-changing treasures: a *Guideposts* magazine, a candle, a leather-bound journal, a fountain pen, rosewater spray, or even a joke book. Plus, my suitcase never leaves home without my traveling altar with lightweight fabrics to throw over any surface, a few candles, spiritual icons, beautiful music, and a CD alarm clock. No matter where I go, I have customized, beautiful surroundings to inspire me.

Add Gratitude and Compassion

Developing positive ways of being—like gratitude and compassion—reveals the More that already exists in life. Gratitude leaves little room for feeling sorry for yourself, a state we often use to justify a soft addiction routine as a supposed "treat" for ourselves. Gratitude raises our consciousness of what is loving and good in our lives. Gratitude can be shown in innumerable ways: saying "thank you"; showing appreciation to those who have helped you; saying grace before meals; appreciating a kiss from your husband or wife; or treasuring an unexpected letter from a friend.

Gratitude opens us to the deeper truth that we are all connected, and compassion keeps the link forged between our hearts and the hearts of others. It reduces our inclination to be judgmental and encourages us to love rather than harangue. Without compassion, when we feel bad about the things we do or feel, we look for ways to escape, and our soft addictions are the perfect answer. Compassion creates greater acceptance of our darker side.

You can add compassion by accepting your humanity, remembering that every person in the world struggles with soft addictions, and by practicing self-forgiveness. This is a life journey and we are here to learn and grow, not to achieve perfection.

ADD ACTIVITIES SPECIFICALLY DESIGNED TO FULFILL YOUR HUNGERS

Like a grocery store stocked with ingredients for your meals, the list that follows is a storehouse of activities to feed your spiritual hungers. At the Wright Institute, students in our learning laboratories use these activities as life assignments. They challenge mistaken beliefs, open new possibilities, and teach new behaviors. Adapt these assignments for yourself, and add ideas for activities that would feed your deeper soul urges. Then you'll have a ready list of additions for creating your Formula for More.

SPIRITUAL HUNGERS	ASSIGNMENTS
To know you exist	Speak up when you feel ignored until you feel acknowledged
	Create a ritual to welcome yourself to your day
To be seen	Show up and express yourself
	Do something outrageous
	Practice stating your preferences
	Dress well and consistently in a way that reflects you
To be heard	Speak up in a meeting
	State an opinion clearly
	Argue with people and challenge ideas
	Sing out loud in public

To be affirmed	Be with people who believe in you
	Ask for feedback from a friend
	Get positive attention five times a day by doing a good deed or greeting someone warmly
To be touched	Get a massage or facial
	Give and receive hugs
	Do a relaxation meditation, tensing and releasing every area of your body
	Ask your lover to hold you or even rock you like a baby
	Cuddle your cat or dog
To be loved	Look for evidence of being loved, cared about, thought about, and held in others' consciousness
	Keep a journal of kindnesses
	Acknowledge to yourself when someone does a caring act for you and record it
	Be with people who understand and appreciate you
To be loving	Perform random acts of love and care
	Write love notes to loved ones
	Do something to further someone's dreams
	Be friendly everywhere you go

To express	Feel and share your emotions
	Express your creativity in dance, art, writing, problem solving, or crafts
	Learn and grow every day
	Share your opinions with others
	Debate an issue
To be known; to be connected; to matter	Share of yourself
	Keep no secrets from your spouse
	Join a group that values truth and honesty
	Seek out feedback
	Be a good friend
	Empower others' dreams—believe in them, support them, encourage them, and keep them accountable
To make a difference; to fulfill your destiny	Be value-added and make contributions in every gathering you attend
	Volunteer for a cause that matters
	Contribute to everyone
To be one with the greater whole	Pray or meditate to be with God
	Develop an active relationship with God or spirit
	Commune with nature
	Go on a spiritual pilgrimage
	Practice feeling like you belong to the brotherhood of mankind

Look for the divine spark in
other people
Live life as a sacred journey
Visualize yourself as a beloved
child of a loving God

ADDING TO YOUR FORMULA

Now that you have been exposed to the wide range of possibilities that you can add to your life, start thinking about your formula. What goals do you have and what action steps do you want to take to move toward your Vision? Pick a few goals and some related action steps that will help you create a life of More. You can begin to enter them in the template at the end of the chapter. Use Morgan's life examples and Tyler's formula to inspire you to possibilities in your own life.

SUBTRACTING IN YOUR FORMULA

Now that you have planned what to add to your life, you can look at what you would like to subtract. At this point in the process, identifying soft addictions to subtract should be easy. Think about the ones you identified in Chapter 4, and add any that you've thought of since.

Subtracting for Morgan began with her soft addiction to zoning out in front of the television after work. Instead, she added a self-care routine that included tucking herself into bed. She reduced her soft addiction to work when she added lunch with friends and planned more activities for after work. Subtracting her self-critical thoughts and anxious moods was perhaps the most difficult, but she found that as she expressed them to others, the reassurance she received reduced their occurrence.

Subtracting is easier when you add something compensatory first, but it can still be difficult to break long-ingrained habits. Here are a few tactics that have been helpful for others.

Subtract Temptation: Identify the Initial Step in the Cycle

What tempts you to lapse into your listless state? What activity precedes sitting down and watching lots of television? What happens right before you start a marathon gossiping session? Whatever it is, identify it and try to avoid it. Change your route to work so that you don't pass the shop where you habitually overspend. Cancel your cable subscription for your television, remove the computer games from your computer, or clean your cupboards of tempting sweets. Any change helps disrupt the soft addiction cycle. We are creatures of habit, and changing even one step of the routine decreases the temptation to indulge in it. The initial step in the cycle can be an especially important item to subtract.

Subtract in Stages

Placing limits on soft addiction routines naturally produces subtraction. Limit the amount of time you give yourself to shop or establish arbitrary parameters, like refusing to work out on any day starting with a "T." You're changing the routine, and reducing the habit gradually.

Morgan added a comforting bedtime ritual to help her subtract her nighttime television watching. But she also subtracted her television watching overall in stages, starting small and increasing the limits as she went along. Staging the limits in this fashion is often easier than setting an ambitious limit right from the start.

Morgan's first subtraction involved moving her television out of her bedroom. She then limited her television watching to two hours each day. She later canceled her ca-

More-sel

"Habit is habit, and not to be flung out the window, but coaxed downstairs a step at a time."

—MARK TWAIN

ble service. She tightened the boundaries by decreasing her television watching to five days a week. She sits with her back to the television in restaurants. With these limits in place, television no longer grips Morgan as it once did. Her boundaries confine the amount of time and energy wasted on an activity that takes her away from her Vision.

Subtract Negative Thoughts

Curbing self-deprecating thoughts and eliminating rationalizations is one of the best things you can do for yourself. This pervasive force of negativity justifies soft addiction routines and undermines your Vision. Subtracting these negative thought patterns creates room for More—more loving, affirming, encouraging, truthful, and empowering thoughts. You might want to revisit Chapter 5 for a refresher course in countering your stinking thinking.

Subtract Clutter and Confusion

It is easier to stay conscious without distractions. Think about what's on your kitchen countertop, dining room table, or your desk. When it's clean and clear, you think twice before messing it up. A vision, by definition, is something we need to see clearly. Living an uncluttered life keeps the More we desire in sharp focus.

Reduce clutter and confusion by cleaning surfaces, organizing drawers, and creating a quiet setting. Start by cleaning one drawer or a small section of countertop. Rather than turning on the television as background noise when you come home, play some inspiring music. Enjoy five min-

More to do

Focus on what is being naturally added to your life—time, money, resources, consciousness, energy, etc.—as you subtract your soft addictions. Create a balance sheet with what you're adding next to what you're subtracting. Use this sheet as a reminder of all the good things you are bringing into your life.

utes of your commute in the quiet, without the radio or CD playing. Get used to being with yourself.

HOW IT ALL ADDS UP TO A PLAN

We can all make our dreams come true by living according to the Math of More. There is no wrong way to do it. Any movement in one area influences another area. The important part is to choose a place to start and then do it.

As you work on your formula, describe your goals in terms of measurable results rather than wishes or vague desires. Action steps should be concrete and doable, and you should choose steps that you are fairly certain that you can accomplish. Keep in mind that any step toward your Vision, no matter how small, generates More.

Pick a time period for your goals of anywhere from a year to a month. If you set a goal for a year, break the goal down further into subgoals you can accomplish in a month. Action steps hold the most power when they cover no more than three to four weeks. If you choose action steps that only take a day or a week to accomplish, you'll recommit, inspired by your small successes.

With all this in mind, you are ready to create your Formula for More. Use these Do's and Don'ts as a guide.

DO'S AND DON'TS FOR A FORMULA FOR MORE

As you plan your Formula for More, the following Do's and Don'ts will help you keep your thinking in the right spirit:

DO'S	DON'TS
Do relate goals and action steps to your Vision.	Don't treat action steps like a heavy to-do list.
Do things that feed your spiritual hungers.	Don't feed your surface wants.
Do have additions.	Don't just have subtractions.
Do add beauty, expression, inspiration, gift developing, compassion, humor, gratitude.	Don't add more soft addictions!
Do plan for success.	Don't plan huge steps.
Do have small steps.	Don't think that any step is too small.
Do enjoy the learning journey.	Don't go for a quick fix.
Do have goals that are measurable.	Don't have vague wishes.
Do have fun.	Don't get too heavy.
Do remember every little step counts.	Don't get overwhelmed.
Do pick just one thing to do, if you will do it.	Don't overload.
Do add support and accountability.	Don't be a lone ranger.
Do keep your Vision before you.	Don't forget you are making your dreams come true!

FORMULATING YOUR FORMULA FOR MORE: A TEMPLATE

Now's your chance to formulate your own formula for a life of More using the template below as a guide. (Or use the template on our Web site, *www.theremustbemore.com*.) You can start your plan now by reviewing the work you've done in the previous chapters. Restating your One Decision, your Vision, and your deeper hungers reminds you that your goals and action steps are not just a to-do list. They are the chance to put your greater Vision into action.

My One Decision:

_____

_____

_____

_____

_____

My Vision:

_____

_____

_____

_____

_____

My Soft Addictions:

_____

_____

_____

_____

_____

My Hungers: Primary spiritual hungers I wish to address

_____

_____

_____

_____

_____

My Additions:

My Goals: What do I want to add in my life to feed my spiritual hungers?

_____

_____

_____

_____

_____

My Action Steps: What steps will I take toward my goals?

_____

_____

_____

_____

_____

My Subtractions:

My Goals: What will I reduce or subtract to curb my soft addictions?

_____

_____

_____

_____

_____

My Action Steps: What will I limit or omit?

_____

_____

_____

_____

_____

EXECUTING YOUR PLAN IMPERFECTLY

Do not concern yourself with perfection. The point is to align your life in the general direction of your Vision. You want the opportunity to learn, adjust, and experience an abundance of life, and that is not possible if you're frozen in some idea of perfection.

Think of it this way. If you fly on a plane from Los Angeles to New York, the pilot follows a flight path, but he does not fly directly on an exact straight line at every moment. He continually corrects course from moment to moment, turning left then right and back again, dealing with different flight and weather conditions. His flight plan doesn't need to account for all the different conditions that come up. View your formula in the same light and allow course corrections on your journey to More.

A Formula for More shouldn't be focused on eliminating all soft addictions. Simply getting rid of an addiction isn't that big a win. Adding more spiritual nourishment into our lives and releasing the hold of our soft addictions is what matters. We are adding sacredness to our lives and creating space for More.

Your Vision can become reality, and the good news is that you don't have to do it all by yourself. You need and deserve support in this quest, and I'm going to share with you the many ways you can enlist this support and draw sustenance from it.

10.

SUPPORT AND ACCOUNTABILITY: A LITTLE HELP FROM YOUR FRIENDS AND YOURSELF

"In order to fight the good fight, we need help. We need friends . . . we need the help of everything around us in order to take the necessary steps toward our goal."

—PAOLO COELHO

No visionary in history ever achieved his or her vision in solitude. Realizing a vision demands more than one person alone can supply. This is a good thing, because it forces you to discover the comfort and joys of support as well as the certainty and direction accountability can provide. The support of others enables you to bring your Vision to life, while the mirror of accountability provides feedback and keeps you going in the right direction.

Without support and accountability, the insidiousness of soft addictions will lure even the strongest among us. A strong support network inspires and encourages. With accountability, we gain checkpoints to keep us on track.

The accountability process explained in this chapter will guide you to choose the right action steps and to establish timelines that include periodic assessment of your progress. It teaches you to build in rewards and consequences.

The support system helps you surround yourself with people to guide you, to encourage you, and to celebrate you as you move toward a life of More.

ACCOUNTABILITY

Accountability means simply that—taking account. Many people mistakenly believe that accountability means punishment for failure. It merely suggests assessing where you are in relationship to your goals. Here are a few ways to build assessments into your Formula for More and avoid sliding back into your soft addiction routines.

Tell People About Your Vision

As soon as you tell someone about your new Vision, you automatically make yourself accountable. Knowing that someone else knows your plans keeps you more aware and honest. Giving words to your Vision helps you to focus on what you're accomplishing and makes you more eager to live up to your declaration. Sharing gives others permission to be committed to your success.

For example, I've told many people that I am writing this book. They've responded with anecdotes about their soft addictions and admitted that they hunger for More. Others send me quotes and articles and wish me well. Just today, one of my students sent me an e-mail with a great quote on spiritual hungers; my niece e-mailed from Italy asking me how the writing is going; and my husband called to check in on me and remind me to have fun with the book. I am happy to be asked, "How's the writing going?" I appreciate being in other people's thoughts. Their knowledge of my goal keeps me moving toward it.

> ### More to do
>
> Discover a new kind of "Tell-a-vision." Tell someone your vision today. Drop it into a conversation or even send an e-mail. If someone asks you, "What's up?" tell them!

Add Time Frames to Goals and Action Steps

Putting action into motion is difficult if you don't make it concrete with commitments like, "By next month, I'm going to spend ten more minutes every day on this truly meaningful activity that connects to the vision I have for myself."

All of your goals and action steps, therefore, should be assigned a time frame. Goals should cover longer periods of time—quarterly, by season, or within a year. Action steps can be planned anywhere from a week to a month in advance. Consider them "alive-lines," rather than deadlines.

When setting time frames, be realistic and don't make too big a leap from where you are now. It's generally not realistic to go from a life filled with soft addictions to one filled with nourishing activities overnight. Unrealistic time frames discourage us and cause us to abandon our plans. When you meet an alive-line, you'll feel rewarded and keep moving forward. So keep them simple and incremental to assure your success.

More to do

What are some of your goals and action steps? List them out and give yourself alive-lines. Put the steps in your date book or calendar. Keep your list with you and check your progress weekly.

Assess Progress with Another Person

Ask someone to check in with you regularly so you can report your successes and defeats. Based on the feedback you receive, you can decide to renew your plan or to readjust it. If you aren't making progress, then adjust your steps. Your buddy can help you strategize.

Design Rewards and Consequences

Accountability encompasses both rewards and consequences. Rewarding yourself when you meet your goals gives you positive incentives for moving toward your Vision. For example, treat yourself to that new play you wanted to see when you successfully curtail your television watching for a month. Read a chapter of that great book you've had your eye on or take a luxurious bubble bath to relax after completing a task that you have been procrastinating about. Plan conscious breaks for yourself and use them to celebrate the completion of your action steps.

Ashley, for instance, had a soft addiction routine of watching too much late-night television. She would often fall asleep in her clothes in the living room in front of the television and wake up rumpled and confused in the middle of night. So, she set up a goal of creating a bedtime ritual that was much more nurturing. If she went a whole week without falling asleep in front of the television, she rewarded herself with a treat to support her bedtime routine—a nice pair of pajamas, a sweet bedtime story, a new candle to light, a calming CD to lull her to sleep. The choices she made not only motivated her to continue working toward her Vision but also helped provide her with the More—more sweetness, more beauty, more peace.

By adding rewards to your action plan, you learn to celebrate your successes. People in soft addiction routines tend to have black-or-white thinking—*Either I completely release my routine or I have failed.* Celebrating the success of each small step helps to reinforce new behavior and reminds you that every step counts despite back and forth movement. Rewards can include breaks, entertainment, or any activity you enjoy.

Be creative and set encouraging, not punishing, consequences for when you fall short of your goals. Plan realistically so one failure does not cause complete abandonment. Take a moment now to write out ideas so that you have a ready list. A consequence could be to journal about your resistance to change, or to call a friend for support. You might also design consequences that keep you aware of the costs of your behavior. For instance, you might write a check to your favorite charity to manifest the financial loss you experience when you are irresponsible with money. Design your consequences to lead you toward your Vision and toward the More.

More alert

Beware of rewarding progress with a soft addiction!

SUPPORT

Remember that part of having More in life means more support—more people vested in your success, more encouragement, connection, resources, partnership, intimacy, and inspiration. Getting and giving support is a beautiful way to meet our spiritual hungers. The universal hungers that we all have are fed through the compassion and honesty of other people.

More to think about

Recall a time when you received emotional support from another person. Remember how you felt when that person listened, offered advice, or demonstrated his or her care for you. Hold the positive feelings of support in your mind to motivate you to reach out to others for help.

Kicking any sort of addiction is easier when you have support. With a circle of insightful friends to talk to, you'll find it infinitely easier to resist the allure of soft addictions. A support network provides real, meaningful relationships as opposed to surface satisfactions. Find people you can trust to give you honest feedback. They'll help you strategize and overcome obstacles as well as engender possibilities to help you achieve your Vision.

HOW TO CREATE SUPPORT

Like many people, you may find the idea of having support attractive but the prospect of finding it challenging. How do you convince your fellow soft addictees to support you in your search for More? How do you meet new people who see the value in a spiritually nourishing life and recruit them to join your support group? There are many ways, and here are some of the most beneficial:

Clear your barriers to support. Many of us learned not to use support in our families of origin. Learn to recognize limiting family patterns and beliefs to open yourself to the possibilities of new types of support.

Discover supporters through new activities. Using the Math of More, you decided to add a variety of nourishing behaviors and activities to your life. It stands to reason that you're likely to meet people involved in these new activities who resonate with your Vision. Perhaps your formula includes going to plays, performances, lectures, or book signings. That could lead to participation in literary clubs, art museums, or a foreign affairs club. You could take up quilting, flying airplanes, or practicing Tai Chi. All these activities will generate a new pool of people draw support from.

Become a student of life. When you are a student of life, you'll cultivate a curious attitude, and you'll find a reason to engage with people who can help you learn. You'll feel more entitled to ask questions and to interview people. You will attain perspective, tips, ideas, and answers. As a student of life, you're open and inquisitive in your explorations and studies of the More. Along the way, you'll create support for yourself.

You'll begin to see everyone around you as wellsprings

of knowledge and wisdom. When you accept that you're not supposed to know everything—that you're a learner on a path—you'll find that you're not embarrassed to ask people for help. You will also begin seeking out people for their talents, as in the following example.

Sherie had a small home-repair business. She longed for more in her life and was keenly aware of the longing. Turning forty, she saw her birthday as a reckoning point. She resolved to learn about the things life offered that she had been missing.

One of Sherie's clients was a busy young working couple. She noticed that this young couple had something more than most. They were honest and affectionate with each other. Spontaneous and playful, yet dedicated and spiritual, they seemed so alive. To step into their home was to breathe a sigh of relief; it felt peaceful, yet fun and inviting. She noticed touches of beauty and care throughout their home and was surprised to see a spiritual altar instead of a television in their living room. This couple was involved with their careers, personal growth activities, and contributing to others. Now that she'd declared herself a student of life, she was able to inquire about how they had carved out what seemed to be such a meaningful life. The couple told her that they had not always lived in such a way. They had learned to change limiting family patterns and manage a number of soft addictions before they found their More. They introduced Sherie to their path and put her in touch with their teachers. Sherie began her own journey of growth and transformation, putting into action her resolution to get more out of life after forty.

Solicit support from family and friends. Not everyone will automatically support the changes you make as you try to create More. In fact, people may make fun of you or treat you with disdain, disbelief, or disrespect. Don't be surprised if some actively undermine your efforts to change. Perhaps they feel threatened by the changes or are in denial about their own soft addiction routines.

Nonetheless, don't keep your desire for More a secret. In addition to resolving your family patterns, explain to your family and friends that you are undertaking something that has meaning for you and that you want their support. Tell them about your One Decision and share your Vision.

Let them know you are creating More in life. From your heart, include them in what you hunger for.

Come to terms with your decision to change. When you are at peace with your decision and maintain great resolve, you'll naturally generate more support and avoid the naysayers. If, on the other hand, you're ambivalent about changing, people sense the uncertainty. They may then reflect your doubts and ambivalence in their comments and attitudes. When you feel more secure about your choices, other people's comments and opinions bother you less. The strength of your One Decision becomes stronger than anyone's negativity. However, prepare for comments like:

> "Why are you doing that?"
> "What do you think you are doing?"
> "What makes you think you can change that?"
> "What difference does that make?"
> "What makes you so high and mighty that you think you're better than us?"
> "You don't hang out with us anymore; do you think you're too good for us?"
> "You're such a dreamer."

To empower yourself around your commitment, it is critical that you allow yourself to feel hurt, angry, or afraid when others don't want to change with you. Remember to express your feelings responsibly but be sure to express them. Trust that you will find people to support you or that they will find you.

CREATE FRESH SOURCES OF SUPPORT

Anticipating negative reactions, you may have a stinking thought like, *Everyone I know is an Internet junkie; I'm never going to get them to approve of what I'm trying to change.* If you can't look to your immediate circle for support, you need to create new relationships with a different circle, whose beliefs and values are more aligned with your own. This isn't as difficult to do as you might think. Here are some easy-to-use tactics to create fresh support.

Talk to People

When most people think of support, they imagine that it has to come from a good friend, spouse, or therapist. While these are great sources of support, don't overlook the power of talking to anybody and everybody. The universality of soft addictions makes it a natural conversation topic. I have talked about soft addictions with complete strangers. I've had stimulating discussions about soft addictions with waitresses, entrepreneurs, flight attendants, CEOs, housewives, ministers, priests, rabbis, tradespeople, beauty contestants, children, grandparents, high-powered advertising executives, homesteaders, home schoolers, and high schoolers. Each immediately shared their struggles or at least said, "I have a friend who . . ."

> **More-sel**
>
> "Keep away from people who try to belittle your ambitions. Small people always do that, but the really great make you feel that you, too, can become great."
>
> —MARK TWAIN

Almost every person has wrestled with soft addiction routines. Some have overcome them and now lead a life of More. Others may have a strong desire to overcome them. Most people are likely to be highly receptive to a conversation revolving around the subject and will provide you with verbal and emotional support as you work to change the way you live.

See People as Partners

Other people can add great richness and meaning to our lives, but only if we consciously see them as capable partners. Too often, we look at people from limited perspectives. In making the commitment to fulfill our Vision, we need to broaden our view of what people can provide us. By shifting our perspective, we increase the odds that they'll provide us with support.

Practice broadening your perception of people. Rather than slapping individuals with a convenient label—Joe, my colleague; my weird Aunt Doris; Sue, my tennis partner—look at them in terms of their knowledge, skills, achievements, character strengths, and so on. Think about people in your life, whether an acquaintance or someone you've known for a long time, to create your resource list. Ask yourself the following questions:

What makes this person special? Is it something he does for his job, something she does as a parent, something he knows that other people don't, something to do with her spiritual capacity or the way she seems so at peace with her life?

How does my particular Vision relate to this person's special quality; what can I learn from him or her that will help me find the More I'm seeking?

More to do

Take a moment to reflect on the people in your life. Choose three people who have a talent or skill in an area you would like to develop. Ask one of them to help you develop this skill.

Give Support

When you give support, you see interactions with others as opportunities for mutual support rather than as chances to gossip or indulge in other superficial exchanges. By consciously reaching out to others, you'll encourage others to reach out to you, creating mutuality.

My husband, Bob, is a master of mutual support. A very intentional man with big dreams, he is acutely aware of his Vision and goals. He also keeps the visions of others in his consciousness. He assumes any conversation is for the purpose of creating More for both parties. As he talks to people—anyone from the UPS delivery person, his seatmate on an airplane, a close friend, a salesman for copying equipment, a valet parker, or a CEO he coaches in leadership training—he engages them in conversation about what is important to them and helps them identify and clarify their dreams. He delights in finding ways to support each person he comes into contact with. He'll solve problems, find resources, and inspire them with possibilities. Through these conversations, he discovers talents or resources that facilitate his own Vision or the vision of someone in his life. Not only does he create mutual support but he also creates a larger resource network that spirals outward, weaving a web of connection and possibility.

> ## More-sel
>
> "Never doubt that a small group of thoughtful citizens can change the world. Indeed, it is the only thing that ever has."
>
> —MARGARET MEAD

Participate in a More Group

While you can create support in many ways, don't underestimate the power of a group of people all going for the More. Encourage the people around you to join you on your path. Look for connections at every gathering: book groups, neighborhood meetings, work teams, Bible study, committees, playgroups, family holidays, sports teams, writers' groups, spiritual groups, and members of your carpool. Post a note in your neighborhood grocery store, coffee shop, or cybercafé.

If you'd like to join or even start a More group, or just receive support and inspiration, log on to my Web site, *www. theremustbemore.com,* to find what you need to start a group of your own, be part of an on-line community, register to start a group in your area, attend a training, or even become a trainer yourself. You can ask questions, share victories, strategize recovery from defeats, be inspired, and find even more ways to More on this Web site. You'll also find chats, bulletin boards, quizzes, soft addiction computer games, Webcasts, and more to encourage and support you on your path.

CONTRACTING WITH OTHERS: TAKING SUPPORT AND ACCOUNTABILITY TO THE NEXT LEVEL

While you will want to talk to as many people as you can about your Vision and plan, contracting with a few key people will provide a higher level of support and accountability. A formal contract will ensure that you both enter into the relationship with a high degree of commitment. It will keep you focused and provide more specific ways to stay accountable.

In the There Must Be More Than This training at the Wright Institute, students contract with each other, monitor assignment accomplishment, share their plans, provide feedback and encouragement, trade battle stories, and report in on what has happened in their quest for More.

Like them, you can use various types of contracts and assignments to help you achieve greater support and accountability.

Equal Trades: Creating Support Buddies

An equal trade contract involves finding someone who is working on the same issue and making a formal commitment to each other. Talk to people to discover who is interested in what interests you. It might be someone at the gym, in your book group, or at the coffee shop. Look for someone who has the same soft addiction routines and is interested in decreasing their dependence on them. Or, you may find an individual who shares your belief that there must be more than this even if his or her routines differ from yours.

Nelson, who frequently engaged in a procrastination routine, discovered that Mark, a member of his health club and an occasional tennis partner, fell into the same habit. Each knew that they spent a lot of time talking about all the meaningful things they wanted to do but never quite got around to doing them, offering one excuse after another. Though their Visions for themselves were different, they recognized that they were both reflexive procrastinators and wanted to shift so they had more time and energy for meaningful activities.

Nelson and Mark made the commitment to take at least one action step a week as part of their contract. For Nelson, this involved doing what he had always dreamed of. He created a lobbying group for companies in his industry. For Mark, it meant getting involved with a local environmental volunteer association and helping them become more effective. They agreed to talk at the end of each week to monitor progress and hold each other accountable. In addition, they agreed that if they weren't making progress, they would take action to get back on track. At the same time, the agreement called for celebrating victories and empathizing about setbacks. Both Nelson and Mark have made substantial progress toward their Visions because of the contract. Mark's lobbying group is set to take off, and Nelson is chairman of the water quality committee. They're procrastinating less in other areas too, filling their free time with meaningful activities they have longed for.

More-sel

"Nothing is more powerful than a great network of support. In fact, you will not be able to break out of the grip of automatic living without the help of other people. Find new friends who are also willing to stand out the wild winds. Create a group of friends dedicated to supporting one another to make the entire group's dreams come true."

—NICHOLAS LORE

Realistically, you may not know someone who shares your soft addiction routines, or you might not be able to find a person interested in entering into an equal trade contract where you both support each other. Therefore, you may choose to ask someone to hold your contract for you. Many people will gladly lend you support and feel honored that you chose them. Select someone who will be encouraging, compassionate, and caring but who will also firmly hold you to your agreements. Tell them your Vision, goals, and action steps, as well as the timeline you created. Check in with them on a periodic basis to account for your progress, to problem-solve when blocked, and to recommit. To let them know the importance of the matter, set up a regular check-in time.

Let's Make a Deal: Trade Strengths and Gifts

You can also contract to trade strengths and resources. This type of contract works best when you ask for support and establish a clear trade agreement. Make it official and it will work much better for both of you. It is really a barter arrangement, and it's important to be clear on the specifics of the trade. If you treat it casually, so will your trading partner, and neither will hold the other accountable. Set a time limit on what you're trading and be willing to renegotiate the deal's terms at the end of the designated time.

This "let's make a deal" strategy is especially effective for married couples or other loving partners.

Scott and his wife, Chris, have contracted for support. They have a meeting over breakfast every Saturday morning and discuss their Visions and goals for the week. They design their plan to include support for each other. Scott is working at being more physically agile and creating a better baseline of health so that he feels more vital. Since Chris is savvy about nutrition and exercise, he asked her for support with his diet and workouts. She tends to overclean the house and indulges in busywork and television addictions. She asked for Scott's support in letting go of her cleaning obsession, having more fun, and being more spontaneous. Scott contracted for Chris to provide a minimum of three low-fat meals a week, and to plan outings like biking or hiking. Scott shares great literature with Chris in place of television and to use as breaks from housework. He also invites Chris to have more fun and lighten up at least three times a week. He tells her jokes, brings home comedies, and sends her funny e-mails. Every week they assess how they are doing and adjust the plan as needed, adding steps to reach their Visions.

SUPPORT IS MORE THAN A TEMPORARY TOOL: THE MANY USES OF YOUR SUPPORT NETWORK

Support isn't limited to someone to talk to when you're tempted to fall back into a soft addiction routine or to hold you accountable for your new goals. People who get More out of their lives have a circle of support that they use in various and creative ways. They're open to help from others, whether it's a friend who's willing to lend them an ear or a professional who is able to help them deal with complex feelings.

Let's look at ways in which you can use support as you embark on your quest for More as well as throughout your life.

Support for the Feelings That Change Brings Up

As you pursue More, you'll find that others can help you validate and express the feelings that emerge. As you remove soft addictions, you remove barriers surrounding your heart and your feelings. Expect feelings of loss. Positive change is still change. It represents a loss of what was. You may feel bratty or angry from time to time as you become frustrated. You may feel more exposed and vulnerable as you strip away your soft addiction routines and become more genuine.

Accept your sensitivities and see your feelings as positive. Others who understand what you are going through are invaluable. They will reassure you that your feelings are legitimate and remind you that you have worked hard to have them.

As you look for support, therefore, seek people who are comfortable with talking about and experiencing feelings. Find individuals who aren't shy about telling you how they feel and seem genuinely interested in having you express your emotions, even difficult ones like anger or fear.

Be aware that you may even feel uncomfortable as some of your emotional supporters respond positively. Accept that these people have your best interests at heart and that you're uncomfortable because of who you are becoming and not because they positively acknowledge your feelings.

You should also be prepared for jealousy and resentment from unsupportive people. Envious and resentful people may try to make you feel guilty about doing so many positive things. They may even mask this jealousy as concern "that you are doing too much." Having the support of others who are not threatened by your success is essential.

Marta, for instance, was attempting to add spiritual nourishment to her life and subtract a variety of routines that were physically unhealthy at worst and mind-numbing at best. As she spent more time listening to music she loved through concerts and CDs, and going for long, meditative walks, Marta found herself experiencing her feelings more intensely than she had in years. Both her happiness and her sadness flowed freely. Marta was scared of these feelings.

In addition, men found Marta more attractive—she had lost weight and seemed more energized and alive. Marta, however, struggled with her feelings about the new men in her life. Though she felt flattered, she also felt more vulnerable than ever before when she was genuinely interested in a guy. She was so threatened by her feelings, in fact, that she started to eat more and put back on the weight she had lost, unconsciously trying to discourage men from asking her out.

Fortunately, Marta recognized that a better alternative was to seek support. She started talking to other people she knew who were overcoming their soft addictions and she reached out to a woman who had season tickets next to her at the symphony. They all affirmed the feelings that she was having, sharing their own experiences. She set up a contract with the woman from the symphony, and they talked once a week, without judgment, about what they were experiencing.

Because of their conversations, Marta gradually stopped viewing her own feelings as abnormal; she recognized that others had experienced what she was going through, and it helped her cope. Instead of gaining weight to protect herself from her feelings, Marta slowly began to accept that there was nothing wrong with her and that intense feelings paved the way toward a more meaningful existence.

> ## More-sel
>
> "Sometimes our light goes out but is blown into flame by another human being. Each of us owes deepest thanks to those who have rekindled this light."
> —ALBERT SCHWEITZER

Vision-Keepers Help You Keep the Faith

As we journey toward our Vision, we naturally question our decision. Most people have doubts, second thoughts, and concerns about what they are doing. Frequently, doubt rears its ugly head: *Why did I say I wanted this anyway? It's too hard. What's so hot about making conscious changes, anyway?* I call this a "chump" conversation. In the clarity of a moment, you make the One Decision and start to create your Vision. Then you run into a difficult moment and have second thoughts. Your resistance comes up in the form of derogatory thoughts about yourself: "What was I thinking? I'm a chump. I actually believed for a second that I could have More in my life." This is a critical time for reinforcements!

Enlist a vision-keeper for yourself. Ask a friend, co-worker, family member, or even a boss to be your vision-keeper. Give her your written Vision and ask her to read it to you regularly. Ask her to randomly e-mail it to you and remind you of it when you are faltering. Call her when you are having doubts. This type of support is essential, especially when you have a big dream and you start doubting it precisely because of its enormity.

I had a dream of creating a retreat and conference center where we could work with people in greater depth without the distractions of everyday life, while supported by beautiful, natural surroundings. I envisioned people growing and mutually empowering one another to transform their lives in this setting. I searched for land for more than three years, looking for something that felt right and was within two hours of Chicago, where we lived. We finally found a beautiful property replete with rolling hills, forests, and native prairie situated around a lake. The buildings, however, were a mess. There was beautiful architectural design, but no one had ever finished the buildings. They were rotting from neglect and water damage. Animals had burrowed into the buildings, mice ran rampant, water poured in the walls. Most of our friends told us we were crazy when they saw the property. They said if we did buy the place, we should torch the buildings. They shook their heads in disbelief.

At the time, we also had a lovely home in an exclusive suburb that we had just redone and decorated. Why would we give that up for this ramshackle place? One of our friends, a founding member of Findhorn, the famous intentional spiritual community in Scotland, knew what could happen when people followed and

More to do

Volunteer to be a vision-keeper for someone you know who is making positive changes in his or her life. Feel the sanctity and honor of holding a vision for another.

built from spirit. She believed in what we were doing and could see our vision clearly. She became our vision-keeper. When we became discouraged and wondered whether we were doing the right thing, we would call her. She reminded us of the importance of our vision and her belief in us. She never faltered in her belief and her stance. She played an essential role in making the big leaps to establish the Prairie Spring Woods Center, which is now flourishing, successful, and serving many people.

Creating a Life Team

Support isn't just for the present but for the future. Achieving More isn't about crossing a finish line and winning the race. It's an ongoing process, and though it's important to have people supporting you as you move toward your goals, it's just as important to have people helping you after you've achieved them.

For this reason, creating a life support team makes sense. In essence, the team consists of committed people living the More. Purposeful, growth-promoting, and inspiring interactions with your team will be the norm. Your interactions will be relaxed, but never casual. Mutual purpose defines all you do.

Most of us, however, don't consciously pick our friends and actively decide who might best help us achieve our vision. As a result, we don't naturally create a life support team. Instead, we surround ourselves with people who like to do the same things we like, which often means we hang out with our soft addiction partners. Celeste is someone who has gotten past this and built a life support team in a highly conscious manner.

Celeste owns a beauty salon. Her clients include television stars, harried professionals, and others who view her salon as an oasis of calm and care. Celeste is aligned to a higher purpose and sees her work as a vehicle for her mission. She doesn't just do a job; she has a true vocation. She feels she provides a spiritual experience for herself and her clients with every service she provides. A mother of two, she is devoted to her husband and is taking college classes to complete her degree. Deeply religious, she is open to all religious traditions. Life is a rich experience for Celeste. Originally from Eastern Europe, Celeste appreciates the opportunities she found here and wants to take full advantage of them. She constantly hears her family and friends saying, "Slow down, you do too much. What are you running around for? How come you don't come to all the family gatherings? Who do you think you are?" They are threatened by her pursuit of the More.

Though she loves her family, Celeste doesn't allow them to hold her back. She picks and chooses family events to attend, and prefers deep contact with the individuals in her nonfamily circle. Socializing and just hanging out isn't enough for her. She wants to connect deeply with people, share goals and encouragement, and talk about things that matter. She loves to be with entrepreneurs making a difference in the quality of their world. They, too, are going for More and know what it takes to do it. Her husband also provides great support for her. He loves the woman she is and shares her pursuit of More. This helps her to manage the naysayers in her life, those who try to discourage her from pursuing her dreams.

Like Celeste, you can assemble a similar life support team. This doesn't mean that you exclude everyone from your life who remains stuck in a soft addiction routine, but it does mean you form a group you can rely on to keep you focused on the More for years to come. To build this team, keep the following guidelines in mind:

Pick supporters. Look at candidates for the team as supporters rather than just socializers. Fun people are great, but that is not the criterion for membership.

Make conscious choices. Be conscious in your choices; don't just fall into relationships or blindly accept someone for your team just because you grew up with her or have worked with him for years.

Expect more. Insist that people bring gifts of More to the party.

Go for depth. Look for interactions with depth, a deeper sharing of life goals, inner yearnings, and strategies to live More.

Change your filters. Be aware of how you screen out people you deem inappropriate or not your type. Using different filters can open you up to new possiblilities for More.

Try the following exercise to evaluate members of your life team and new possibilities:

1. List the people in your life whom you want to evaluate.

2. Create a set of five to ten values/criteria for rating these relationships. Your criteria might include truthfulness, playfulness, gives good coaching, or any other quality you value.

3. Rate each person on each of your criteria, using a scale of one to five, and then total each person's score.

You may be surprised to find that your highest quality support comes from unlikely people in your life.

Seek Role Models and Inspiration

As you become more aware of conscious living and get more involved in meaningful, soul-inspiring activities, you're bound to encounter people who serve as models for a life of

More. They are the people who treat life as a sacred journey and have learned to manage their soft addictions. Finding these role models—who provide the support of "I did it, and you can too"—is not as difficult as it might seem. When you open your mind as well as your eyes, you'll see that role models surround you.

Look for people who are alive, vital, and who make a difference. Watch for emotionally available individuals who possess these qualities. Pay attention to people serving mankind in some way or who seem blessed with an abundance of energy and wisdom. Read biographies of people who have achieved More in their lives; watch the media for stories of individuals making a difference in the world.

One of the most inspiring lives of More is chronicled in *Acres of Diamonds* by Russell Conwell. Conwell believed that all the riches in life lie within each of us and are available if only we seek them. Through his life as a soldier, a minister, an attorney, and the founder of Temple University, he demonstrated the power of making the One Decision and of living his life in accordance with it.

Consider, too, the life of St. Ignatius of Loyola. Ignatius was a wealthy, vain party animal who spent much of his time carousing with friends. After receiving a leg wound in a skirmish, Ignatius fretted over the look of his wounded and potentially misshapen leg in the fashionable tight stockings of the day. While recuperating, the only reading material available was *The Lives of the Saints* and the Bible. To his surprise, the people he was reading about fascinated and elevated him. They led much more exciting and inspiring lives than he. St. Ignatius followed the stirring of his soul to make what we might call his One Decision. After his recuperation, he laid down his sword in an all-night vigil to Our Lady of Montserrat and continued on the path that led him to sainthood.

Going for More doesn't mean that you seek sainthood, but the example of people seeking a deeper life can have a positive effect on your own life. Be inspired, not daunted, by people going for More. Recognize that you have the same hungers. They have made their One Decision and harnessed their life energies in pursuit of More, and so can you.

DRAW SUPPORT FROM SPIRIT/GOD

Praying to a higher power and deepening your relationship with spirit are tremendous sources of support for people trying to live a life of More. You can seek this support in any way you choose. For instance:

Have conversations with God or your definition of spirit. Ask for help in adding positives and resisting soft addiction temptations.

Feel your prayer. If you say the Lord's Prayer ("Our Father . . ."), let yourself really feel the words "lead us not into temptation."

Pray for guidance. Ask to be shown ways to develop and use your gifts.

Let spirit be your guide. Develop spiritual practices and bring God or spirit more directly into the fabric of your daily life. Make God your confidant and best friend, as close as a lover, as familial as a sister or brother, as accepting as a divine, loving parent.

Reveal your heart. Tell God about your hungers and the yearnings of your heart.

As I write, I often type a prayer and then listen to the response of spirit. It connects me with a sense of something greater. I no longer feel alone; I feel that I can draw upon vaster resources than my own. Do the same thing when you're struggling with your soft addiction routines and attempting to pursue more meaningful activities and moods. Say a prayer about your struggle and leave yourself open to a response.

<table>
<tr><td>

More to do

Many studies now indicate the efficacy of prayer. Ask someone you know to pray for your success in creating More in your life. Watch what happens!

</td></tr>
</table>

Look for spiritual support in the natural world. Lie on a bed of soft grass, feel the wind caress your skin, gaze on nature's rivers, lakes, and oceans. Walk in the woods, lunch in the park, work in your garden, applaud the sunset, and look for constellations in the night sky. Sense the rhythms of nature and seek the wisdom encoded in the seasons and growth cycles. The natural world inspires and enlightens us in ways that people can't. Raising our awareness of nature and attuning to its rhythms will steer you away from your old routines and toward a more fulfilling life.

PUTTING SUPPORT INTO ACTION

Now that you've learned how to garner support, it's time to revisit the Math of More. In the Formula for More, you created goals and action steps that added activities and behaviors aligned with your One Decision, and subtracted activities and behaviors that pushed you toward your soft addictions.

Now you'll put your newly created support system into action. Revisit each goal and action step you selected. For each action step, determine your reward or consequence, and agree on specific alive-lines. Plan your support in your Formula for More. (Remember, you can use our Web site, *www.theremustbemore.com*, for support, too.) Use the examples in this chapter to guide and inspire you. Commit to being supported and write down by whom, when, and how you'll be supported. Sharing your life with others who support you is living More.

GIVE YOURSELF THE GIFT OF SUPPORT

No question, asking for support can make you feel vulnerable. Whether you're offering up a prayer or requesting that a friend form a contract with you, you're revealing yourself to someone else. This can be scary. Receiving support, too, creates more intimacy in your life. While we all say we want closeness, we may be scared of people knowing us that well. We may be afraid of setting up accountability, thinking *What if I fail? What if I don't measure up?* We may also feel like we're not worthy of receiving help from others. We're afraid of being a burden or bothering someone else. Or perhaps we feel like we should be totally independent and not need anyone.

As difficult as all these things may be, recognize that you not only need support but that you deserve it. The more we take on, the more support we need. To ask for help and sustenance is not a sign of weakness, but a sign of resolve, intent, and purpose. Think about the support Olympic athletes need. They have coaches in all aspects of their sport—chiropractors, choreographers, massage therapists, orthopedic specialists, sports psychologists, nutritionists, and business managers—to support their bodies, minds, and spirits. Going for More means participating in the spiritual Olympics. For athletes, support is a sign of their dedication. Let the support you generate be a sign of your resolve to have More in your life.

11.

DETOURS ON THE ROAD
TO MORE . . . AND HOW TO
GET BACK ON THE PATH

"It's not whether you get knocked down;
it's whether you get up again."

—VINCE LOMBARDI

The road to More is a winding road—a road that goes deeper, not just farther. Unlike predictable soft addiction routines, the road to More forges into new experiences and challenges. So it's easy to become sidetracked. The purpose of this chapter is to encourage success on your journey to More by preparing you for bumps in the road, getting stuck, breakdowns, roadblocks, backsliding, and blowouts.

Not that breakdowns are bad, or blowouts necessarily to be avoided. The people I coach discover that there are opportunities and lessons in each detour. Bumps generally lead into new opportunities and territory. Wrong turns can actually enrich your journey.

Reading about a trip and going on one are two different things. Books, by their very nature, make any process appear simpler and more straightforward than it actually is. As you've read about the skills involved in living More—from articulating a One Decision to identifying an addiction to developing a Vision and so on—you've begun to use your

Formula as a mental checklist detailing what you have to do to get the More. It might seem that if you do A, B, and C, you'll arrive quickly at the More and stay there.

The skills of this book aren't a simple step-by-step process that you easily complete and then you are done. They are skills to build and apply throughout your life. These aren't eight easy steps and then you are "fixed"—in any sense of the word. You are not broken, so you don't need to be fixed. These skills are guides to living that you can apply over and over again to create a life of More. The more you apply them, the More life you'll have. The skills are suggested in a certain order, but once you have learned them, you can use any of them at any time to support you on the road to More.

Life is much richer and more varied than the pages of a book. Achieving More happens only after you've tried, failed, gone down dead ends, hit reverse and then gone forward, and cleared formidable hurdles. You may even realize your Vision, experience the More, and still fall back into your soft addiction routines. While such stop-and-go progress can be frustrating, it can also enhance your appreciation of the More by deepening your experience.

You'll need guidance to keep you on the road to More and to keep a detour from becoming a dead end. At the end of the chapter, you will learn to use these five Rules of the Road to More to encourage your success by supporting you through the inevitable frustrations of your journey.

Rules of the Road to More:

1. Be Prepared
2. Don't Panic
3. Ask for Help
4. Keep Going
5. Learn and Grow

Jake's story illustrates the types of bumps you can encounter and the types of breakdowns that can happen. By following his journey, you will learn to recognize and anticipate common pitfalls on the road to More. You'll see Jake's triumphs and mistakes and how he benefits from both. You'll become aware of the challenges ahead and how the Rules of the Road to More can keep you on track despite the obstacles that arise.

JAKE'S JOURNEY

Jake was well on his way to creating More in his life. He'd done the right things: he made his One Decision and admitted his soft addictions of power fantasies, risk taking, overspending on clothes and gadgets, being cool, and what he called being "on the prowl." He loved the feeling of being on the edge in his entrepreneurial wheeling and dealing and liked the high that came from taking chances in many areas of his life. But he also knew this feeling offered, at best, fleeting satisfaction.

Jake began what he thought would be a journey toward More by deciding to tone his body and get rid of the "bumper" around his waist. He thought that his appearance was the only barrier to true happiness for him.

Yet Jake ultimately realized that the impact of his soft addictions extended far beyond carrying around a few extra pounds. No matter how much sharper he looked, how much stuff he bought, how many women he dated or big deals he closed, Jake couldn't shake an emptiness inside. He never felt he had enough, made enough, or was enough. Jake's daily routines were spiritually bankrupt.

After attending a men's weekend at the Institute, Jake saw his obsessions more clearly. He began to understand how his fixation on appearance, his drive to own things, his pursuit of an adrenaline rush, and his escapes into power fantasies were rooted in feeling inferior, particularly to his father and other successful men. No new Ferrari, trophy girlfriend, or million-dollar deal could ever truly assuage this feeling.

It took this realization for Jake to discover the spiritual hungers beneath his soft addictions—his need to be seen, affirmed, and loved. Once he owned up to these hungers, Jake could start taking steps toward More. He reined in his recklessness in business, curbed his spending, and started spending more time with new, supportive friends who appreciated Jake for who he was, not what he had. Jake met strong men who challenged his superficiality. He shifted his focus in business from just closing deals to actually enjoying contact with his clients. As Jake's natural gregariousness and good humor emerged, clients started looking forward to his visits. Once he stopped trying to act rich and followed his Formula for More, Jake found true wealth in a life that was rewarding and affirming.

Yet after a while, Jake began inexplicably doing things that took him away from the More that he had achieved. He started isolating himself and stopped getting together with his friends. He took daredevil risks while skiing, and began overspending again. In place of the positive activities he'd developed, Jake started substituting new soft addictions, like surfing the Web for hours.

What happened? Life was giving Jake much that he'd dreamed of, but he didn't feel entitled to all the emotional rewards. While Jake loved the joy, bliss, and deeper connection to spirit that he felt, he hadn't prepared himself for the increased awareness and onslaught of feelings that emerged as he stopped numbing himself with soft addictions. He was becoming acutely aware of his pain, fear, and anger. And when Jake felt angry, he couldn't sustain his "good ol' boy" demeanor—nor do "good ol' boys" cry much.

Frightened by the new feelings of intimacy and closeness he was experiencing, he pulled away from his new friends and started hanging out with his daredevil, gadget-obsessed cronies again. He seemed to drop off the planet, screening his calls and never returning those from his supportive friends.

The moment of truth came the morning of a triathlon for which Jake had been training many weeks. His new friends gathered at a local restaurant to see him off and cheer for him along the route. But Jake never showed up.

One of Jake's most supportive and loyal friends was Patricia. When Jake missed the triathlon, she stopped by his house. At first Jake didn't want to see her, but she refused to leave until he let her in. As they talked, Jake claimed he didn't truly care, that this journey toward More was stupid, and that he'd been better off before he began discovering himself. For a long time, Patricia just listened. Then she started patiently questioning Jake about his choices.

Gradually, he started to see for himself where and why he'd panicked. As Jake admitted his fears to Patricia, he relaxed. He saw that he hadn't been bad or weak but simply scared and ill-equipped to deal with his fears. His willingness to learn, grow, and pursue More reasserted itself. With Patricia's help, Jake remembered his One Decision and the things he had enjoyed about his life of More, including his warm friendship with her. In a candid and tender moment of clarity, he admitted that while he had deeply missed her, he hadn't felt comfortable with or deserving of the warmth and caring she shared so freely with him. He didn't think he'd earned it. He saw that he'd been overwhelmed by the new richness of his life and the wealth of friendship that had come his way.

So Jake's breakdown became an opportunity for breakthrough. When he realized what was going on, he experienced an "aha." Jake had used soft addictions to hide from his emotions. As he challenged those addictions and began creating a life of more meaning and connection—the life he wanted—deeply buried feelings surfaced, not all happy ones. Seeing that he was going through predictable highs and lows permitted Jake to accept himself, reorient to the More, and discover additional spiritual hungers—to feel secure, to feel safe, and to trust. With these hungers firmly in mind, he began learning the skills to go about meeting them more directly. For instance, he learned to talk more about what he was feeling, which allowed others to support him and provide reassurance and comfort. He started dating women who were warmer and more available emotionally, instead of just good-looking. He shared more with everyone, and expected more in return.

In retrospect, Jake was able to identify his detour as a learning experience. He saw how dealing with his "feelings overload," as he called it, had called for skills he didn't possess yet. He wouldn't have been aware of his negative beliefs or had the opportunity to shift them without the detour he took. Understanding that he could expect detours prepared him to deal with future challenges, recover more quickly when they occurred, and even learn from them as they arose.

> ## More-sel
>
> "What gets in your way can take you to someplace new."
>
> —SARAH EAST JOHNSON

BREAKDOWNS BECOME BREAKTHROUGHS

When you follow the Rules of the Road to More, you can turn each breakdown into a breakthrough. Each time you make progress and then backslide, you have opportunities to learn more about yourself and identify the new skills you need to learn. Things looked pretty bleak for Jake before he turned his breakdown into a breakthrough, with Patricia's help. Jake didn't know that breakdowns are a normal part of growing and changing. So when he started feeling and behaving in unfamiliar ways, he assumed that something was wrong.

It wasn't. A child learning to walk falls many times before finding his balance and mastering this new skill. If every child waited to try walking until he could do it without stumbling, we'd crawl all our lives. In the same way, breakdowns are predictable missteps as we learn to lead bigger, more complex, less predictable lives.

From his breakdown, Jake learned to expect more ups and downs and to be compassionate with himself when they came. Breakdowns aren't failures; neither are they passes to give up. They teach us where we're vulnerable in our growth, so we can develop particular skills to support ourselves.

When you discover your motivation for returning to a soft addiction routine or unearth the underlying hunger that caused you to backslide away from your Vision, you peel away the built-up layers that obscure the deeper, more essential you and your inner motivations. You'll have more data about your life, and you'll see more of what you need to learn to succeed on the journey. Remember, the win in this game is consciousness. The more aware you are, the more you will be learning and winning the game.

CHALLENGES ON THE ROAD TO MORE

There's a little (or a lot) of Jake in all of us; namely, fears of the unknown, shutting down in the face of them, backsliding, and losing our way for a while. Although challenges can come in many varieties, there are three common forms of challenges on the road to More. Keep these challenges in mind as we see how Jake responded and broke the basic Rules of the Road when he needed them most.

Challenge: More Feelings

If we are successful in subtracting our soft addictions, we will be successful in unearthing more feelings—pleasant ones

and difficult ones, but most important, *strong* ones—which are nothing
like the dull, muted feelings we had
when we were sleepwalking through
a softly addicted life. Sometimes, on
the way to our goal, we return to soft
addiction routines to numb the freshly
uncovered feelings. If you view feelings negatively, you may find yourself

falling into this trap. Unlocking our negative beliefs about
emotions, learning to be with our feelings, to befriend them,
and express and resolve them are key to staying on the Road
to More.

Challenge: Unknown Territory

Because soft addiction routines are just that—routines—
they keep us in known and predictable situations. The road
to More is a road into the unknown. Going into the unknown can be overwhelming and threatening, especially if
we are unprepared and have not developed strong naviga-
tional skills. Without soft addiction routines, we experience
variation and uncertainty and a very different sense of space
and time. This unknown new territory can also provide
many uplifting and energizing experiences. However, we
need new skills to negotiate the unknown.

Challenge: Your Feelings of Self-Worth

Your beliefs about your worth can be challenged as you create More in your life. If you don't feel deserving, it is hard to
pursue More. Your successes, ironically, may expose mistaken, unconscious beliefs that you're unworthy, undeserv-
ing, unloved, or unlovable.

We yearn for success without realizing that victory can

be just as destabilizing as setbacks. Tears of celebration and frustration are equally possible on the road toward More, and can be equally unnerving. Jake backslid because he felt uncomfortable with all the feelings that his success was bringing him. He turned back to his bad habits to help him check out emotionally.

BLOWOUTS ON THE ROAD TO MORE

Not all of us will have a blowout the way Jake did. We're more likely to get stuck, stall, or backslide and then rouse ourselves to get moving again. Blowouts happen when the implications of living differently overwhelm us. Blowouts are extreme, erratic reactions caused by reliving old experiences, reawakening buried fears, or releasing old pain. They are rarely predictable and often take place following high levels of achievement. Frequently, a blowout is a reaction against a radical redefinition of the self, which can happen as we reach for More.

For Jake, training to be a triathlete was changing his definition of himself. He saw he had the capacity to be successful as both a competitor and as a friend. The support his new friends were giving him was proof he could be this different person. Combining such high expectations with Jake's relatively immature life skills and newly emerging emotions was too overwhelming. Blowouts most often occur when individuals do not have a strong relationship with their feelings. Rather than face this new force in their lives, they may instead panic and flee.

PLAYING BY THE RULES

Here's how the Rules of the Road can help you deal with these challenges. Applying these rules doesn't mean you'll never hit rough patches as you go for More. But they can ease a backslide, or shorten the time you spend trying to get back on the path if you lose your way.

Rule #1: Be Prepared

People who succeed at any adventure usually do a good job of preparing. And don't kid yourself, no matter how well things are going now, there will be bumps along with successes and plateaus on the journey to More. I have learned from backpacking and global travel that anticipating problems is key, because things often happen to me that I wasn't expecting. Yet if I've prepared well, I usually have enough tools and resources to deal with surprises.

In its early years, the Peace Corps found that nearly half of its volunteers bailed out prematurely on their two-year assignments abroad. Research revealed that the volunteers were not adequately prepared for the challenges posed by their new environments. When the Peace Corps added classes to teach volunteers how to anticipate problems and succeed in a new culture, the number of those returning home early became negligible. Later, budget cuts forced the Peace Corps to drop this training, and volunteers once again began leaving the program before completing their assignments. In other words, prepare and beware of too much too soon. If you don't put a strong foundation under your structure, it can crash.

Jake, for instance, failed to prepare for problems. As he dropped his soft addictions and changed his life, he felt like a tourist in unfamiliar emotional territory. His usual landmarks were missing. Everything around him looked different, felt different, and seemed to operate by different rules.

Because he hadn't expected daily emotional surprises, Jake hadn't come prepared with tools to help him understand or care for himself in his newly vulnerable state.

Like a tourist heading for unfamiliar parts, Jake could have prepared himself by taking classes or talking to others who'd visited this state of being. He could even have picked a buddy to check in with regularly for information and reassurance. By choosing to do it all himself, Jake increased his chances of getting homesick for his old soft addictions when he felt overwhelmed by the newness of his changed life.

Rule #2: Don't Panic

If you find yourself returning to a soft addiction routine or doing something else far removed from the Vision you've created, don't panic. Backsliding and breakdowns are part of the process. Knowing this, you'll be prepared for one of the great emotional challenges on the road to More—namely, dealing with your fear.

Jake's panic showed up as a return to old patterns of addiction. Unable to admit even to himself that he was afraid and upset, Jake didn't recognize his blowout until Patricia helped him see it.

The greater our fear, the stronger and more unreasoning our attraction to old habits of being and thinking becomes. The fact that Jake didn't even want to hear from people he cared deeply about shows how powerful his fear had become. Above all, he just wanted to soothe himself, and he was willing to backslide enormously to do that.

Until we can name our panic, it runs us. Being able to accept what frightens us is like shining a light under the bed. What we think are scary monsters turn out to be little more than our own imagination. Checking out our worst fears with others can also be very reassuring, for we see we aren't alone. Everybody gets scared, and usually about the same things.

Rule #3: Ask for Help

Jake seemed to flee help rather than asking for it. We must wonder if the thought even occurred to him. Remember our earlier discussion of support? If you are nearing a hazard on the road to More, this is when you'll need support! Get used to asking for guidance and help early in the game, when you seem to need it less. If you use support consistently, it is already there when you most need it. Men are notorious for refusing to stop for directions when they get lost. Yet women are guilty of not reaching out sufficiently on the road to More, too.

And while we're talking about support, it's vital that you think carefully about whom you ask for help. I cannot overemphasize the importance of reaching out to winners rather than losers in the game of More when you need guidance. Some people, sensing your vulnerability, might use it to drag you down. Jake's fear took him off the path until Patricia reawakened his willingness to learn, grow, and pursue More.

If someone asked us to lift an enormous stone or tree, we wouldn't hesitate to ask others to help. Yet we often try to shoulder enormous emotional burdens alone. If we were navigating a new country, the first thing we'd do is ask for route guidance. But we think we should be able to transform our lives and navigate new relationships without help.

It can be hard to admit, "I just don't know." As adults, we think it's our job to have the answers. Jake felt increasingly vulnerable as he ventured further toward More. He imagined that everyone understood life better than he did. The irony of asking for help is that we often find others feel just as vulnerable as we do—and out of the shared vulnerability, wonderful support can grow.

Rule #4: Keep Going

Not only did Jake fail to keep going, he had no mechanisms to help him persist and alert him of the dangers of slipping.

More-sel

"Even if you are on the right track, you'll get run over if you just sit there."

—WILL ROGERS

Even when you feel yourself sliding backward, it's important to keep going. You never know what agent of Providence is waiting to help if only you do your part and persist.

Cling to your goals, even if you have to start over in moving toward them. Establish some simple action steps in your Formula for More that become regular routines and support your new lifestyle. You may fall off the wagon from time to time, but so what? So does everyone. Dust yourself off and climb back on.

Jake would have helped himself if he'd set up more routines that countered his soft addictions. For instance, working out in the evenings with covoyagers would have cut into

More-sel

"Never, never, never give up."

—WINSTON CHURCHILL

his time to surf the Internet. He also made the error of losing contact with the friends who supported him.

Even if you backslide or get stuck, keep up your disciplines. Keep going even when it seems pointless. Chances are that, with patience, your efforts will be rewarded. Eventually your clarity will return enhanced, and with it, renewed determination.

Rule #5: Learn and Grow Along the Way

More to do

Keep a daily growth journal. Write down your challenges, lessons learned, the skills you developed, or future activities needed to develop them.

Wherever you are on your path, there is a lesson to learn or a sight to see. This is especially true when you feel stuck, in a breakdown, or freaked out. You can always take in new information. Learning is knowing something today that you didn't know yesterday, and growing is developing the ability to do something you couldn't have done if you hadn't had a certain experience. Learning and growing make us much more resilient and better able to respond to the bumps in the road.

Being able to see the lessons that every hit, wrong turn, dead end, and backslide presents takes skill. Because he was a relative newcomer to living with More, Jake needed Patricia to help him see his lessons and tap this mind-set.

At the root of our breakdowns on the road to More is our difficulty in accepting ourselves. At the deepest level, this is a question of faith rather than psychology. It is a question about our view of our place in the world. Are we embraced by a loving universe? Are some people more worthy than others?

The next chapter presents the key to shifting our beliefs about our place in the world. It reveals the source of both my faith in genuine emotional expression and my belief that we are loved and worthy. Join me in the next chapter as we explore four loving and transformational truths and discover how they can inspire and support each of us on our path to More.

12.

THE FOUR LOVING TRUTHS

The road to More is a spiritual path, and all who travel it embark on a sacred journey. Following this path leads us deeper toward life's essential truths.

I'd like to share a discovery with you that helps me both when I am at loose ends and in the peak flow of joyful creativity. These simple yet profound truths came to me as I was in deep prayer, meditating on divine love. I call them the Four Loving Truths.

When I've doubted myself or lost my way, they've guided me back to the path. When I've struggled, they've brought me back to myself. When I've needed inspiration, they've made it clear why I was following the path of More. When I live in accordance with these Truths, I have no need for my soft addictions. Spirit sustains me instead.

As you learn to recognize and live by the Four Loving Truths, you will notice the quality of your life changing. A richness and a sense of belonging will be revealed to you as you travel the road to More. It's not necessary to believe these precepts in order to benefit from them. You just need to operate as if they are true. As you align with the Four Loving Truths, you will open yourself to the possibility of More in your life.

As you've learned, mistaken beliefs about your feelings and your self-worth can send you off on detours from the road to More. Orienting to the Four Loving Truths corrects these mistaken beliefs. Living in accordance with these

Truths rather than with mistaken beliefs lessens the need for soft addictions.

Now let's turn to these Truths, discover the inspiration they offer, and look at how you might align your life with them.

THE FIRST LOVING TRUTH:
YOU ARE LOVED

You are loved beyond your own imagining. You may not feel it, know it, or even believe it, but the truth remains that you *are* loved. You are a beloved child of a loving universe. Nothing you can do will make the love go away, for it is your birthright. Is there anything we want more than to be loved? Is there anything that we fear more than the possibility that we are not loved? Our fears are groundless. What we most wish for, we already have. Love is abundant. It is we who block the reception of love, who believe we are not loved, or lovable, or who feel as if we can never get enough.

When you align your life with this Truth, you can experience total satisfaction. You will discover how your life transforms when you can access the infinite love of spirit each moment that you live.

We can trace much of our pain and suffering to the belief that we are not loved and that we are unlovable just as we are. We think we have to earn love and we don't feel that we are able to be good enough or perfect enough to be loved enough. Nothing is further from the truth. Love is not something that can be earned. It is an abundant resource available to all of us, all of the time.

It isn't that love isn't available; it is that we are not available to love.

Our hunger to be loved and our mistaken belief that we are not loved lead us to seek refuge in soft addictions. We think we will be more lovable if we have the great new car or the designer clothes. We think others will think we are worthy if we gossip and share the secrets of others. We exercise for hours daily to be fit enough to be lovable. We feel unloved and soothe the feeling with a soft addiction, blunting our hunger. We go to the Internet for a false connection. We overspend, overeat, acquire, hoard, collect, and amass substances and activities. Our mistaken beliefs about love affect every aspect of our lives and the lives of others.

Many of us did not get the attention or kind of care we needed or would have preferred when we were children. We may have decided then that we were not loved or lovable or that there wasn't enough love to go around. Although these conclusions, made from a younger point of view, are understandable, they don't have to be our operating principles today. Just because some of the people in our early life were not good at showing us love and attention doesn't mean that we have to decide that we aren't loved. We can make another, better choice.

The First Loving Truth corrects the mistaken belief of unworthiness and of being unloved. When we live this truth, we don't need to participate in costly rituals of trying to be cool enough, smart enough, handsome enough, rich enough, or fit enough in order to be loved. Instead of turning to numbing addictions, we can soothe ourselves and be comforted when we feel blue or lonely by opening up to the greater truth that we are loved.

Contrary to a popular mistaken belief, being loved is not a feeling. Being loved is a decision. Having someone love you is not a panacea for feelings of lack, unworthiness, and pain. For example, I know that I am loved, but I do not *feel* loved all of the time. My husband loves me deeply and tells me daily. He believes in me and does whatever he can to help me achieve my dreams. He compliments me (he calls me gorgeous every day) and shows his love for me in many ways. It saddens me that I don't always let his caring in or don't always feel the depth of his feelings for me.

It is a form of stinking thinking to identify a feeling and ascribe meaning to it. It is called emotional reasoning. *I don't feel loved, therefore, I am not loved,* is a stinking thought. A corrected thought is, *I am loved. I'm simply not feeling it right now.*

We often have unrealistic pictures of what being loved looks like. We think things like, *If he loves me, he'll buy this for me.* Or, *If she loves me, she will read my mind.* Or, *If I am loved, I will feel on top of the world.* We have pictures of what we think love should look like and feel like and when they don't match, we decide we aren't loved. For example, if I thought love was always gentle and kind, I would miss the love and concern that pours from my husband when he confronts me with the straight truth. Even when things don't look or feel the way you think they should, there is love.

When we decide we are loved, we begin to look for evidence of it. Because of the power of self-fulfilling prophecies, we tend to act in ways that confirm our current beliefs. If we change either our beliefs or our actions, we can shift the cycle. As you make these changes, you will feel more acceptance, more love, and more hope. Even if you can't seem to feel it in the moment, you will still see the evidence. Not unlike learning new words, your awareness increases, then your command of language is increased: The words were there all along. You'll probably even attract more respect and positive attention because of the shift in your belief system, because you hold yourself as loved and deserving.

By redefining love, you will see that love isn't just romance. Love has to do with caring and holding each other close in your hearts. Evidence of being loved can range from a spouse's loving look, to a parent's stern admonition, to a chore done for you when you didn't ask, to a coworker asking you how your mother is doing after her recent fall, to a boss giving you tough, constructive feedback that will help you develop your potential.

Simple pleasures and the ability to cherish them can also be symbols of love. You can see evidence of being loved in gifts of the universe—a glorious sunset, a cleansing rain, the shimmer of the northern lights, the sunny faces of daffodils on a spring morning, or the twittering of birds at dawn. The magic that comes from human beings—an athletic triumph, an exquisitely prepared meal, a painting by Monet, the artful finishing work of a master carpenter, the perfectly executed document by your assistant—can all be seen as signs of a loving universe.

THE SECOND LOVING TRUTH: LOVE AND PEACE ARE THE LEGACY OF PAIN

Riding on the wave of your pain are the gift of peace and the gift of love. As you open up your heart to feel your pain, you open yourself to receive love and peace. Peace follows pain, like the sun follows the storm. The charge builds, it is released, and all is calm. Cleansing like the rain, sorrow washes your heart and peace and love remain. Bountiful love and peace flood into the tender sanctuary prepared by the vacating pain.

We have mistakenly believed that pain is the opposite of love. We haven't realized that pain and other emotions actually lead to love and can be seen as parts of love. In addition, peace is not the absence of pain but the result of the acceptance and expression of pain. Peace awaits expression. It only arrives when we express what is in our hearts.

Inner peace does not depend on perfect circumstances or the absence of conflict. We experience peace even in the midst of chaos and upset if we are in touch with our hearts and release our pain. As we open our hearts to the feelings that reside within, we find ourselves. Knowing our inner state brings us closer to ourselves, to others, and to spirit. And when we are in contact with ourselves, we can feel the peace of truth.

Our mistaken beliefs about pain cause suffering. We resist pain, thinking that there is something wrong with it or wrong with us that we feel hurt. We may also believe that we can't handle pain. As a result, we mask our pain, we act "cool," or we numb our hurt with soft addictions. By resisting pain, we create a condition of suffering rather than a deep healing experience of our true pain. We create internal upset, anxiety, and a feeling of unease. We don't feel the pain fully and release it.

Pain differs from suffering: pain is inevitable while suffering is optional. Everyone feels pain, sadness, and hurt. Suffering, though, occurs when we have feelings about our feelings, when we revisit our pain again and again. We feel sorry for ourselves because we're hurting or we're mad because someone hurt us. We're upset about being upset. Often we fail to address the pain directly and it persists unrecognized. We are in pain underneath but are only aware of a vague feeling of upset. Suffering is a surface phenomenon. Instead of fully releasing the feeling underneath, we resist it on the surface with our soft addictions. We feel blue, cranky, or angry, or perhaps we act out inappropriately.

It's not surprising that we become attached to soft addictions that dull our pain, even though it means giving up love and peace. We make this terrible sacrifice because we resist our pain, mistakenly believing that it is ugly and renders us unlovable. The opposite is true. We will not feel seen, accepted, and loved without sharing our hearts, which means accepting our pain.

Accepting and expressing your pain is crucial. It does not matter if you express it in words, tears, sobbing, or any other way; it will lead to peace. Ideally, your expression will match the intensity of your pain. In other words, sobbing is a different expression from weeping; the latter may not release enough of the pain to create a sense of peace. Watch a baby to see how her release of feelings brings resolution and peace. When a baby feels upset, she cries fully and the feeling completes itself. In the next moment the baby smiles and coos until the next wave of feelings comes through her. This is how it can be for adults if we allow it.

Intimacy and love only come to a heart open to pain. A heart that shares pain is a heart that shares love. Love and peace are the legacy of pain. When we share our pain we open ourselves to the love of others, to the love of our self, and to the love of God and the universe.

THE THIRD LOVING TRUTH: FEELINGS ARE DIVINE AND TO BE HONORED

Encoded within you is a deep sensitivity, designed to provide you with exquisite information that allows the expression of the deepest truth of your soul. It is through our feelings that we experience spirit, the greater essence of life. Feelings are the universal human language, a conduit from heart to heart, transcending our outer differences and connecting us to all.

We become most human and alive when we cry our tears, laugh our amusement, yell out in anger, shake with fear, reach out with love, and bubble over with joy. Feeling these feelings, naming them, and being in relationship with them in the here and now is the way to a full, vibrant life.

When we deny our emotions, we become depressed, anxious, and even physically ill. We may act out inappropriately rather than expressing them responsibly. Being hurtful, mean, ill-willed, or irresponsible are examples of our dark side's misuse of feelings. Even worse, such a feeling-avoidant attitude causes us to miss the wisdom and aliveness encoded in our emotions. We miss the flow of energy within us. We miss the connection to our hearts, to the hearts of others, and to spirit. When we misuse or cut off our feelings, we miss their ability to lead us to the next level of exploration.

Expression of a feeling often leads to a new discovery of

who and what we are. As we ride the wave of our feelings, we arrive at new understandings, and we express things we never knew. Sometimes we don't know what we think or can't define what's inside until we begin to express the feeling. Expression of the feeling then leads us to new territory where we become something that we weren't before. This process keeps us from being stagnant, from repeating the same thoughts and reactions. It is how we grow. It is what helps us create ourselves.

Without our emotions, we would not be human. Our emotions connect us to every other person. Through them we understand ourselves and one another. We may not share beliefs or have the same thoughts, but our emotions are the language of all humankind; they transcend culture, beliefs, race, age, sex, or any artificial division. All of us hurt, hope, love, sorrow, and rejoice in the depths of our hearts.

Our feelings express truly the deepest parts of ourselves. They reveal and define us. They guide us to express, to heal, to connect, to worship, and to love.

THE FOURTH LOVING TRUTH: GIFTS ARE GIVEN TO YOU TO DEVELOP AND USE IN THE SYMPHONY OF LIFE

You have been endowed with gifts to cultivate and to offer to the world. Each of us is blessed with gifts, and all gifts are valuable. As you express your gifts, you express an aspect of creation that could not exist without you. Embark on the sacred quest to discover, develop, and contribute your gifts. It is your deepest purpose to magnify and manifest your gifts. The world will be in harmony once we all develop and use our gifts collectively.

Accepting that we all have gifts, we can join the quest to discover them. We needn't be limited by mistaken beliefs that we are not talented, or that others are special but not us, or that it is showing off to share our gifts. Convincing ourselves that we lack any real gifts or have nothing to contribute leaves us with an aching void that we often fill with soft addictions. Our fear of failure and our perfectionist approaches bar us from fully engaging in life. We are willing to just get by in order to distract ourselves from our fear. If we believe we have nothing to contribute, we don't fully engage in life and we seek solace in soft addictions. Since we only discover our gifts by engaging in life, we may miss finding the gifts we surely possess.

Our gifts can be anything from artistic ability to mechanical aptitude. Whether it's a penchant for gardening, an empathic heart, a healing presence, an infectious sense of humor, solving computer glitches, being a supportive friend, or being a gifted hostess or ace organizer, we each have many gifts and many ways to contribute to the world.

As you set your Formula for More in motion, you learn to lead your life by looking for ways to develop and offer your gifts. You see new possibilities in your life and you see multitudinous ways to contribute. You then offer the wisdom of your unique experiences, ways of thinking, insight, knowledge, and skills. You live passionately, all the while expanding and sharing your gifts.

The failure to realize and develop our gifts is perhaps the greatest cost of our soft addictions. When we make our One Decision, we rid our lives of soft addiction routines and we raise consciousness. Freedom unleashes our potential. When we assume that we have gifts, we start to look for them. We are more willing to try different things to discover our aptitudes and abilities. Once we see our potential, we take more pride in learning, practicing, and honing our gifts. We become more tolerant of our learning curve.

When we accept this Fourth Loving Truth we begin to see how we can contribute. We all hunger to matter and make a difference. Developing and using our gifts gives us that chance. Our gifts aren't limited to the traditional definition of talents—artistic talent, athletic talent, and so on.

They flow from our feelings and perspectives, our very essence. It might be empathy and understanding borne out of your own difficult circumstances in life. It's possible your gift is the ability to see the best in others. Maybe you can make others laugh or can dance with innate rhythm. Perhaps you have a mystical access to spirit or a determined will. Perhaps you are driven to complete things and can be counted on. Perhaps your gifts include a talent for organizing, cleaning up, making a beautiful space, repairing appliances, quelling a disturbance, or inspiring others. Any contribution you make is a gift.

Once we see that we all have gifts, we know that we do not need to be good at everything. We can freely make use of others' gifts. Your spouse possesses gifts you lack. You have exactly the skill your coworker needs to finish his project. He has the gift you need to interface with the other departments. Our teams and partnerships become swirling centers of creativity, with each person offering his or her unique gifts. We begin to crave diversity because it brings more to the table. Others have perspectives, backgrounds, and skills that we do not have and which complement ours. Diversity isn't then a mandated concept, but a heartfelt desire to bring the best possible gifts to bear.

By developing and offering your gifts, you grow. You become more skilled and more fulfilled. Something new is created and brought into the world. The creativity you express through your gifts empowers you to add meaning to your life and to the lives you touch.

LIVING THE FOUR LOVING TRUTHS

The Four Loving Truths reveal to us the love and wisdom of the universe. They clarify why we've been given spiritual hungers. Just as we are encoded to feel physical hunger so that we eat to sustain our physical body, we are encoded with spiritual hunger so that we seek the nourishment that causes our souls to flourish. As we follow the path to More, we come to know the differences between a soft addiction and spiritual nourishment.

It is my hope that the Four Loving Truths will inspire you as you travel the road to More. The Truths respond to the lament "There must be more than this." Yes, there is More—more love, consciousness, energy, resources, fulfillment, satisfaction, contribution, connection, feelings, life experience, adventure, and discovery. The Four Loving Truths are the essence of More. They informed and inspired every step of this book. May they inspire you and inform every step of your heroic journey to More.

THE HEROIC QUEST
FOR MORE

"The good fight is the one we fight because our
hearts ask it of us. In the heroic ages—at the time
of the knights in armor—this was easy. There
were lands to conquer and much to do. Today,
though, the world has changed a lot, and the
good fight has shifted from the battlefields
to the fields within ourselves."

—PAOLO COELHO

Inspired by the Four Loving Truths, armed with the skills for
More, and aware of the possible missteps, you are now
equipped to voyage into the land of More. Like any epic
journey, it is both fraught with difficulties and imbued with
tremendous rewards. It is a hero's journey and a journey that
makes heroes.

In myths and fables, the hero ventures off to discover his
own way. He doesn't follow the common path. He seeks
something worthy of his efforts, and proves his courage in
continuous tests. He doesn't always attain victory. But he
continues on the quest, learning, developing, and growing
along the way. This classic hero's journey is very similar to
the one you'll be going on in your quest for More.

The path awaits everyone, not just a special few. Setting foot on it helps life become an adventure rather than a series of routines. Seeking More requires character and bravery, and the process itself helps bring out these positive traits. From the moment you make your One Decision, you are on your way to becoming a hero.

FIGHTING THE GOOD FIGHT

As you develop the skills in this process, prepare yourself to fight for a more meaningful life. Your soft addiction "demons" won't go gently into that good night. You must identify and exorcize them. Don't underestimate their power or how unconsciousness renders you vulnerable to them. Therefore, be prepared. Traveling the road to More is a noble endeavor, worthy of preparation.

The path to More is a long campaign. It is not just winning one battle but being willing to engage in continuous skirmishes. I often refer to the people who have done this training as "warriors"—Conscious Warriors. Their quest is not just something to get over or be done with. Each and every conscious choice counts. Each and every step in alignment with their One Decision is a battle won.

While you may experience some setbacks—i.e., falling back into a soft addiction routine—you'll be able to achieve many victories that will keep you moving toward your goal. Don't take these victories for granted, even if they seem small. Be aware and congratulate yourself on achievements. Exult in taking another route to bypass your favorite coffee shop. Triumph in eating half a candy bar instead of the whole thing. Recognize that offering your gifts to another, becoming more sensitive, and allowing a pure feeling to flow through you are victories. Revel in the success of reading great literature instead of the tabloids. Celebrate limiting your Net surfing by walking in the park before work or singing a hymn. Buying flowers for yourself and feasting on their beauty is an accomplishment. Listening to beautiful music as you get dressed in the morning is a triumph.

GUARDING YOUR GAINS

When you have achieved something, guard your gains. As a warrior of consciousness, guard your moments of hard-earned awareness from the onslaughts of unconsciousness. Once you have created more awareness by clearing away some of your automatic behavior, become increasingly protective of your clear space. Don't give ground easily. Be constantly on the alert to add more spiritual nourishment to your life.

Recognize, too, that you're going to be faced with many choices along the way. In fact, one choice often leads to another. You decide to meditate instead of lapse into a self-pitying mood, but then you have to decide how long to meditate and about what. You have to choose whether you're going to meditate the next night as well. Use your One Decision to guide you through the maze of choices.

While at times you're going to be discouraged, challenged, and doubtful as you make your choices, don't forget that all this comes with the territory. You're a hero, and by definition, heroes have to overcome setbacks and self-doubt in order to triumph.

Fortunately, heroes don't have to face their challenges alone. As you'll recall, King Arthur had his Knights of the Round Table, Don Quixote had Sancho, and the Three Musketeers had one another. They shared codes of honor, behavior, and training that made success more likely. Battles are better fought with armies. Triumphs are better realized with friends. Knowing that others are on the path with you can help sustain you in your search for More.

The students at the Wright Institute have access to people who can help them during every step of the process, and this helps them through the rough spots. If you lack this access, you should be aware that it's not all going to be smooth sailing. Join with others to create a support group and log on to our Web site, *www.theremustbemore.com*, so you can be encouraged and celebrated.

THE REWARDS ARE MORE THAN WORTH IT

Even though dangers abound, the journey is abundant with immense rewards. I have helped many Conscious Warriors learn to manage their soft addictions and achieve More, and they have benefited in numerous ways. Just managing their soft addictions liberates them. They gain the gifts of time and energy because they're no longer mindlessly glued to the television, locked in pointless daydreams, or hiding out in their rooms. They acquire insight about themselves and others. They laugh at themselves when they make mistakes and can see the humor in these situations. They are more aware of each moment and can derive meaning and satisfaction from all the small things that make up a day, rather than drift through life in a haze. Relationships become deeper and more intense, and a sense of spirit touches their lives.

It's tremendously gratifying when people realize that these rewards far outweigh the struggles they go through. They understand that as they create space in their lives by shifting negative behaviors, blocks to further freedom show up. It dawns on them that they've tried to fill their hunger for More with soft addictions and now they have the opportunity to fill it with truly satisfying behaviors and accomplishments.

CREATING A WORLD OF MORE

The road to More is not only a path to personal fulfillment, it is a path that can revolutionize our world. Carlos Castaneda affirms the hero's path of More as a reformation and a revolution:

I came from Latin America where intellectuals were always talking about political and social revolution and where a lot of bombs were thrown. But revolution hasn't changed much. It takes little daring to bomb a building, but in order to give up cigarettes or to stop being anxious or to stop internal chattering, you have to remake yourself. This is where real reform begins.

You are becoming a revolutionary—one who lives in new ways. This then is a revolutionary war fought by Conscious Warriors. You are engaged in battles for consciousness within yourself and in the world. You are revolutionizing your internal landscape and revolutionizing the world around you.

MAKING A DIFFERENCE, CHANGING THE WORLD

Living a life of More is both for you and all the people around you. Many of the people I work with find More by contributing to others, making a difference, and having an impact. In a very direct way, their pursuit of a more fulfilling life involves helping others. In an indirect way, their quest for More contributes to a better world because they are becoming more empathic, spiritual individuals. Their transformation adds a little bit More to the world.

If we were all increasingly aware, our world would transform itself. We would meet our spiritual hungers directly, designing our lives to meet our deepest needs. We would know that we had the power to create our lives, instead of just reacting to situations.

"Without heroes, we are all plain people, and don't know how far we can go."

—BERNARD MALAMUD

Our world needs more heroes—people who are willing to do the right thing, make the hard decisions, and stand up for the highest principles and values. The more aware people are, the better their decisions will be. We need people who model a different way of living so that others can draw inspiration from them. We need brave souls who are willing to listen to their own hearts and inspire others to do the same.

Imagine a time when everyone fights for more love, more connection, more spirit, and more fulfillment rather than for territory. This would be a world where all people would live according to the Four Loving Truths—knowing that they are loved, developing and offering their gifts to the world around them, expressing their emotions responsibly, and honoring the revelations of their hearts. This would be a place of balance and harmony, a place we all dream about.

You can help create this world. You may start on the path to More to feel better, but in the process you *become* better and our world becomes better. You create a living example and help to affirm others who want to live a more meaningful, significant life. You develop more awareness and generate more truth around you. You share and contribute your gifts, making the world a better place.

As you go forth, I'd like to leave you with some words to sustain you on your journey:

You are about to begin the hero's journey. Travel well on the quest. A life of More is your birthright. Know the vast resources that reside in you and are provided for you in the world. You have raised the battle cry of There Must Be More Than This. You are fighting the good fight, fighting for More. And by doing so, you are becoming a hero of our modern age. It is in your hands that our future lies. You are a living example of the power of the human spirit, creating hope and possibility for others. Together, may we create heaven on earth, a world of More.

ACKNOWLEDGMENTS

The writing of this book has brought me More!

I have been blessed with the love, caring, dedication, encouragement, support, and hard work of many tremendous people. It is my hope that each of them receives in even greater measure the love and caring they have so generously poured into this book and me.

My particular thanks to the Conscious Warriors—those dedicated students of the Wright Institute for Lifelong Learning who live More and have inspired this book through their examples. No longer compulsively watching television, poring over catalogues or magazines, overshopping, mindlessly surfing the Net. . . . They are instead connected to themselves, their loved ones, and spirit, and are influential leaders in their families, businesses, and communities, creative forces in their world. It is my wish that everyone can now experience these changes in their lives and also experience the outrageous laughter, fun, compassion, encouragement, and inspiration we have shared in our More groups and trainings.

Deepest appreciation is due to all the students at the Wright Institute; working with them is an honor and a delight. Not only do they continually create More for themselves but also in their worlds. I love what we are creating together and feel blessed to be on this journey with them. To the staff and faculty of the Wright Institute, past and present, I am deeply grateful, particularly to Barb Burgess, Kathy Schroeder, Angie Calkins, Christian Marks, Asha Josephs,

Maria Wood, Sandy Mauck, Jillian Eichel, and Jennifer Panning, for their dedication, hard work, care, and especially for their belief in More and in me. If everyone could be surrounded by people who live the tenets of More and apply the skills in their daily work life, what a world we would have!

To Bruce Wexler, Ela Booty, and Christina Canright, I bestow my gratitude for their talents in editing, proofreading, design, and production to bring this book into being.

Love and honor to the women of SOFIA, the Society of Femininity in Action, for their ever-present love and support and their deep care of and adherence to the tenets of this book. They have held this book in their hearts and helped birth it into being. And to Women's Leadership Training, my deepest thanks for selfless service, late-night laugh fests, and around-the-clock heartfelt support and hard work. What a joy it is to lead such magnificent women and to be inspired by their dedication.

Blessings to Gertrude and Rich Lyons, Stanislav Smith, Don and Denise Delves, and Tom and Karen Terry, who believe in More and share their resources to ensure that others experience More. May their generosity and dedication be rewarded a thousandfold.

For those students of the Summer Spiritual Training 2002, I share my ardent appreciation for their immense creativity, hard work, and good fun. I say "wow" to their amazing example of creativity and productivity—what is possible when people come together for a higher purpose! Their vast love and care are imbued in this book.

I sing praises to our Web site and marketing team, Collin Canright, Mike Willis, Dave Stamm, Clay Garner, Anne Lieberman, and Doug Belscher for appreciating the playground and helping more people have the fun of playing on it.

Thanks to my agent, Stephanie Kip Rostan of Levine Greenberg Literary Agency, for believing in this book and escorting it into being. I so appreciate her care and dedication, and our talks about the bigger things of life!

Kris Puopolo, my editor at Broadway Books, has earned

innumerable kudos for her instant recognition of the premise of this book, skilled editing, and dedication in shepherding it with her focused intent and care. I thank the crew at Broadway publicity, sales, and marketing, Suzanne Herz, Brian Jones, Catherine Pollock, and the great sales force, for their enthusiasm, creativity, and support.

To Arielle Ford, publicist extraordinaire, whose generosity and advice led me through mazes and opened many doors, my thanks.

Thanks to my British nanny, Andrew Harvey, who used the considerable force of his personality and intellect to convince me of the importance of getting my work in print. Blessings also to Victoria Schuver-Song, who helped me sing my song in this book. Sincere gratitude to Virginia Rogers, Freya Secrest, and Jim Morningstar for being vision-keepers.

Loving thanks to Marge Wright and to the memory of Mort Wright for their loving example of More and teaching Bob about love and possibilities so that he could share it with me and thousands of others.

In memory of my parents, Dick and Gene Sewell, who showed me the opportunity of service, excellence, and breaking barriers so I could live a life of More. May your legacy of service continue.

To all those who have touched me and blessed this book, named and unnamed, I send heartfelt thanks.

Most especially, thank you to my beloved husband and partner, Bob, without whom this book would not exist. Empowering me to write this book, he supported me every step of the way. His devotion, commitment, creativity, love, and vision inspire me every day of my life. For his inspiring example of living More and his dedication to creating More for everyone around him, I am immensely grateful and honored to share my life with him.

With deepest gratitude to the divine spirit that sources all.

Paris, September 2002

ABOUT THE AUTHOR

Judith Wright, educator, trainer, life coach, and seminar leader, founded the Wright Institute for Lifelong Learning with her husband, Bob, after twenty years of developing innovative, inspirational personal growth programs. The Wright Institute is based in Chicago, where Judith and Bob help people fulfill their potential in the areas of Work, Relationship, Self, and Spirit. Judith began developing and teaching the Soft Addictions workshop over twelve years ago. She is a frequent speaker for events like the Whole Life Expo and SingleFest, for groups like the Association of Humanistic Psychology, the Junior League, and the National Association of Women Business leaders, and for corporations such as Bank One and AC Nielsen. She has blazed many new trails in personal growth, founding SOFIA (Society of Femininity in Action), a cutting-edge women's organization; leading pilgrimages to sacred sites all over the world; and developing many creative and dynamic trainings and programs for couples, individuals, and groups.

Judith Wright can be contacted by telephone at 1-866-MOREYOU or by e-mail at *contact@theremustbemore.com*.

development through consciousness, responsibility, and life-long learning. Courses include living More at work, in sales, at home, in relationship, and while parenting, as well as in spiritual development. Visit the More Web site, *www.theremustbemore.com*, to join the on-line community and see the array of chats, games, products, CDs, and other tools to aid you on your journey to More.

You will find additional offerings at the Wright Institute's Web site, *www.WrightLearning.com*, including our potent leadership training, career development, entrepreneurs' support, and other courses for your successful work life, as well as intimacy, parenting, and communications training for couples and families. We are particularly excited about our cutting-edge women's and men's empowerment training, couples' and conscious singles' activities, and our robust personal development and transformation curriculum. Our spiritual development courses and pilgrimages to sacred sites around the world are attended by people and clergy of all faiths, as well as by those on a secular path who are interested in higher purpose.

There is nothing I love more than helping others live to their highest potential. Let me hear from you. Tell me how you are creating More in your life, both your struggles and your victories along the way. If you would like to contact me for public speaking, training, coaching, or other personal development activities, you can e-mail me at *contact@theremustbemore.com* or call 1-866-MOREYOU or 312-645-8300.

ABOUT THE WRIGHT INSTITUTE FOR
LIFELONG LEARNING, INC.

Love Fully
Laugh Loudly
Pray Often
Feel Deeply
Express Fearlessly
Play Hard
Work Joyously
Commit Totally
Touch Tenderly
Live Consciously©

These words inspire us in our commitment to More at the Wright Institute for Lifelong Learning, Inc., where we are blessed to pursue the More personally and professionally as we serve our students and those we coach.

For some time, our students, staff, and faculty have wanted me to share our work in a format beyond the Institute. This book is my first venture sharing our journey to More in print. My husband, Bob, felt that soft addictions are a good starting point, since they speak to all of us, especially those willing to look at ourselves head-on.

Only one of the many ways we learn and grow at the Institute, *There Must Be More Than This: Finding More Life, Love, and Meaning by Overcoming Your Soft Addictions* brings into focus the Institute's approach to personal and spiritual